MW01708071

AMAR CHITRA KATHA

Illustrated Classics From India

Over 86 million copies of over 400 titles sold worldwide!

Amar Chitra Katha is a collection of illustrated classics that retell stories from Indian mythology, history, folktale and legend through the fascinating medium of comics. Over 430 stories from all over India have been told in this series that has been endorsed by educationists and recommended by teachers the world over.

Through a masterful blend of commentary, dialogue and illustration, Amar Chitra Katha presents complex historical facts and intricate mythology in a format that would appeal to children. They not only entertain, but also provide a fitting introduction to the cultural heritage of India. In a country so vast and varied, the series also serves as a medium for national integration, by introducing young readers to the rich cultural diversity of the country and highlighting the achievements of local heroes.

Amar Chitra Katha comics are like family heirlooms, passed down from generation to generation. These timeless illustrated classics are now also available online on www.AmarChitraKatha.com. Start your own collection today!

IBH

INDIA BOOK HOUSE

 Reprinted: September 2006 ISBN: 81-7508-179-1
Published and Printed by India Book House Pvt Ltd, Mahalaxmi Chambers, 5th Floor, 22 Bhulabhai Desai Road, Mumbai 400 026, India.

Illustrated Classics From India

Raman of Tenali

The triumph of wit over might, of brain over brawn, is a recurring theme in literature. Sometimes, like in the fable of David and Goliath, the gigantic Goliath is defeated with a sling and stone. But more often, like with Tenali Raman, it is done with nimble wit.

Tenali Raman was a Telugu poet and a jester at the court of King Krishnadevaraya of Vijayanagara. He was renowned as the "Birbal of the South" and many stories, which have passed into folklore, are attributed to him. Some of these are obviously invented to show his ready wit, like the one about his encounter with Goddess Kali. This story describes the series of events that first bring the poor young lad Ramalingam of Tenali to the court of King Krishnadevaraya.

Script: Kamala Chandrakant Illustrations: Ram Waeerkar

RAMAN OF TENALI

IT WAS A LIE BUT THE SADHU BELIEVED HIM. HE FELT SORRY FOR THE YOUTH.
IF THAT IS SO, I'LL TEACH YOU A MANTRA* TO INVOKE THE GODDESS MAHAKALI. WHEN SHE APPEARS, ASK HER TO BLESS YOU WITH GOOD HEALTH.
I'LL LEARN THE MANTRA ALL RIGHT — BUT IT'S PLENTY OF FOOD I'LL ASK FOR. THAT IS THE BLESSING I NEED.

BEING CLEVER, RAMALINGAM OR RAMAN AS HE WAS KNOWN, SOON LEARNT THE MANTRA.
GOOD! NOW GO TO THE TEMPLE TONIGHT. SIT BEFORE THE IDOL AND REPEAT THE MANTRA A HUNDRED THOUSAND TIMES. THE GODDESS WILL THEN APPEAR.
AS YOU SAY, SIR.

THAT NIGHT, MUTTERING THE MANTRA TO HIMSELF, RAMAN RAN TO THE TEMPLE.

* CHANT

HE CLOSED THE DOOR AND BEGAN REPEATING THE MANTRA.
AFTER HE HAD DONE SO FOR THE HUNDRED THOUSANDTH TIME —
I AM PLEASED. I WANT TO BLESS YOU.
IT WAS THE GODDESS! THE MOMENT RAMAN SAW HER, A FUNNY THOUGHT OCCURRED TO HIM AND HE BEGAN TO LAUGH.
HO! HO! HO! HA! HA! HA! HO! HO! HO!

THE GODDESS WAS FURIOUS AT THIS IRREVERENCE.
IMPERTINENT BOY! HOW DARE YOU! STOP THAT LAUGHTER AT ONCE!
HO! HO! FORGIVE ME, GODDESS! BUT — I COULD NOT STOP THIS ONE NOSE WHEN I HAD CAUGHT A COLD. WHAT WOULD YOU DO, I WONDERED, IF YOUR THOUSAND NOSES RAN!
THE GODDESS COULD NOT HELP BEING AMUSED.
IT CERTAINLY WOULD BE FUNNY IF MY TWO HANDS WERE TO BATTLE IN VAIN WITH MY THOUSAND NOSES!

* JESTING POET

WHAT YOU SAY IS TRUE, MY BOY. SO I OFFER YOU ANOTHER BOON.
THIS GOLDEN CUP CONTAINS THE SWEET MILK OF LEARNING...
...AND THIS DIAMOND-STUDDED ONE-THE SOUR CURDS OF WEALTH.
ONE OF THEM SHALL BE YOURS. NOW YOU CHOOSE.
BOTH.
WHY IS THE GIFT OF WEALTH OFFERED IN THE FORM OF CURDS?
BECAUSE WEALTH IS SELDOM ATTAINED BY PLEASANT MEANS.

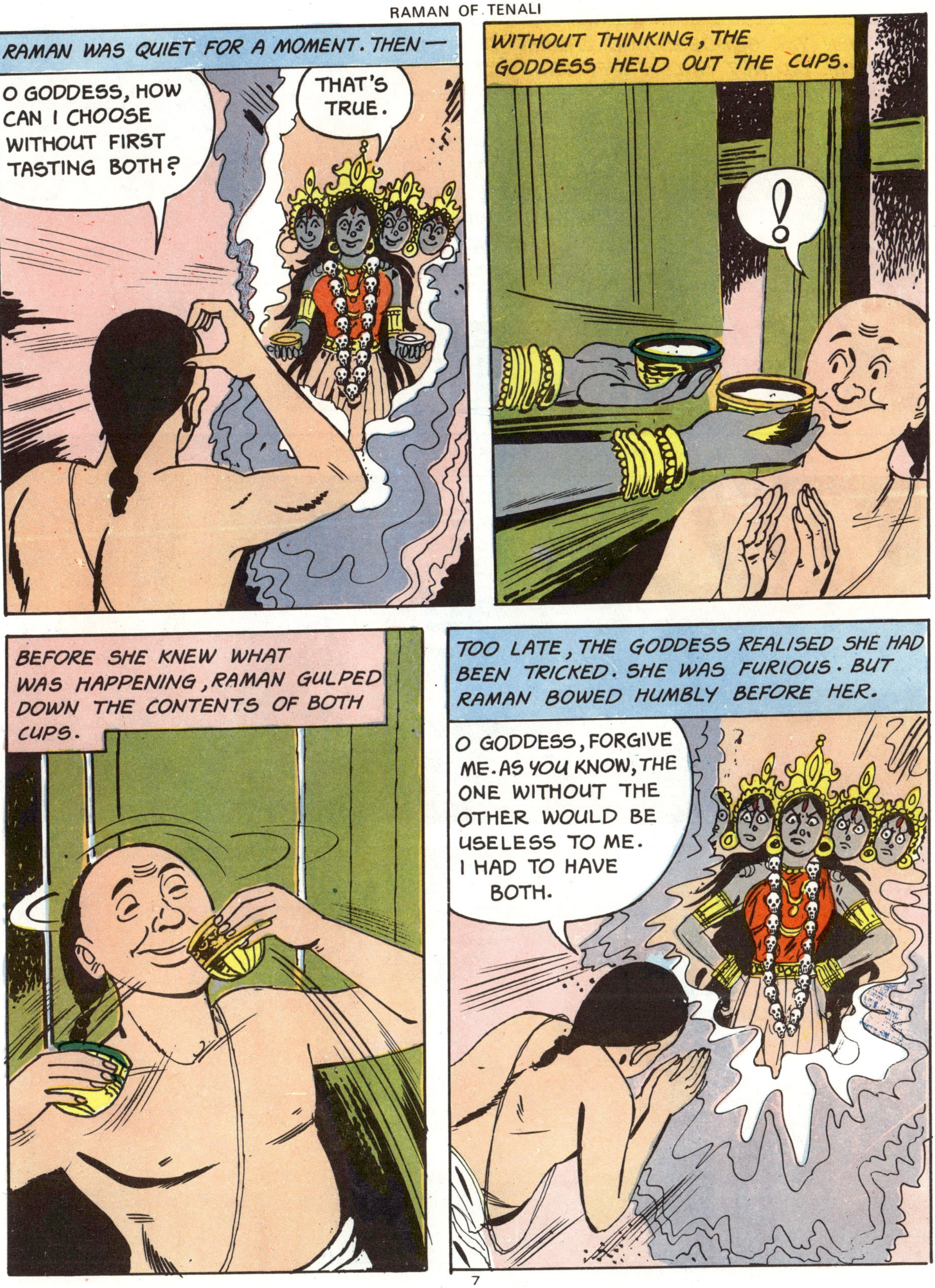
RAMAN WAS QUIET FOR A MOMENT. THEN —
O GODDESS, HOW CAN I CHOOSE WITHOUT FIRST TASTING BOTH?
THAT'S TRUE.
WITHOUT THINKING, THE GODDESS HELD OUT THE CUPS.
!
BEFORE SHE KNEW WHAT WAS HAPPENING, RAMAN GULPED DOWN THE CONTENTS OF BOTH CUPS.
TOO LATE, THE GODDESS REALISED SHE HAD BEEN TRICKED. SHE WAS FURIOUS. BUT RAMAN BOWED HUMBLY BEFORE HER.
O GODDESS, FORGIVE ME. AS YOU KNOW, THE ONE WITHOUT THE OTHER WOULD BE USELESS TO ME. I HAD TO HAVE BOTH.

BY THEN THE GODDESS HAD CALMED DOWN AND SHE DID NOT FIND IT DIFFICULT TO FORGIVE HIM. BUT —
NOW THAT YOU HAVE BOTH GIFTS, YOU SHALL BE WITTY AND WEALTHY; BUT YOUR PROSPERITY WILL ALSO BRING YOU JEALOUS ENEMIES.

QUITE PLEASED WITH HIMSELF, RAMAN TURNED HOMEWARDS.
I WENT TO ASK HER FOR FOOD BUT RETURN WITH HER MOST PRECIOUS BOONS. I'M LUCKY!

AS HE LAY ON HIS BED—
THIS TINY VILLAGE, TENALI, IS NO PLACE FOR A MAN OF MY ATTAINMENTS. I MUST ENTER THE COURT OF VIJAYANAGARA.

THE NEXT DAY WHEN HE SPOKE OF IT TO HIS FRIENDS —
ARE YOU MAD, RAMAN ?
THE PALACE IS NO PLACE FOR RUSTICS.
THOSE HEFTY GUARDS AT THE GATES WILL THROW YOU OUT.
RAMAN KNEW WHAT THEY HAD SAID WAS TRUE BUT HE WAS NOT DETERRED.
I MUST GO TO VIJAYANAGARA. ONCE THERE, I AM SURE TO FIND A WAY OUT. BUT LET ME FIRST FIND A PATRON IN VIJAYANAGARA.
RAMAN SPENT HIS DAYS WONDERING HOW TO GET A PATRON. THEN SUDDENLY, ONE DAY —
WHAT'S ALL THE COMMOTION ABOUT ?
DON'T YOU KNOW ? THE RAJGURU* HAS COME FROM VIJAYANAGARA TO WORSHIP AT THE SHRINE OF MANGALAGIRI.
RAMAN WAS OVERJOYED.
I KNEW IT WOULD HAPPEN. I KNEW LUCK WOULD COME MY WAY.

* KING'S GURU

RAMAN FOLLOWED THE RAJ-GURU TO THE SHRINE.
SIR, MAY I HAVE THE PRIVILEGE OF SERVING YOU?
AND WHO, MAY I ASK, ARE YOU?
WHEN RAMAN TOLD HIM —
WHY NOT MAKE USE OF THE IGNORANT VILLAGE BUMPKIN?
ALL RIGHT, I AM ON MY WAY TO THE RIVER TO BATHE. YOU MAY CARRY MY TOWEL FOR ME.
SIR, I TOO HOPE TO BELONG TO THE COURT OF VIJAYANAGARA, SOME DAY.
WELL, WHY NOT? BUT WHAT WILL YOU DO THERE?

I'LL BECOME THE COURT JESTER, SIR.
IMPERTINENT FOOL! DO YOU THINK IT IS SO EASY TO ENTER THE COURT?
ALL RIGHT. YOU MAY COME TO VIJAYANAGARA AND WE'LL SEE.

BELIEVING THAT HE HAD FOUND HIMSELF A PATRON, A FEW DAYS LATER, ALONG WITH HIS OLD MOTHER AND HIS YOUNG WIFE, RAMAN ARRIVED AT VIJAYANAGARA.
I'LL GO TO SEE THE RAJGURU TOMORROW. I SHOULD HAVE NO DIFFICULTY IN FINDING THE HOUSE OF SUCH AN IMPORTANT PERSON.

EARLY NEXT MORNING, HE WENT TO THE RAJGURU'S HOUSE. HE STOOD BEFORE IT IN AWE.
IF THE RAJGURU CAN LIVE IN SUCH A MANSION, HOW RICH HE MUST BE! AND HOW MUCH RICHER THE KING!

MEANWHILE, THE RAJGURU HAD SEEN RAMAN FROM ONE OF HIS WINDOWS.
WHY! THE FOOL HAS INDEED COME!
HE SENT FOR ONE OF HIS ATTENDANTS.
THERE IS A MAN LURKING IN THE COURTYARD. HE SEEMS TO BE A THIEF. TURN HIM OUT.
BEFORE RAMAN KNEW WHAT WAS HAPPENING, HE WAS OUT ON THE STREET.
SCOUNDREL! YOU WOULD ATTEMPT TO SNEAK INTO THE RAJGURU'S HOUSE, WOULD YOU!
B-BUT HE ASKED ME TO COME... SAID HE WOULD HELP ME...

A CRESTFALLEN RAMAN SPENT THE NEXT FEW DAYS WANDERING AIMLESSLY ABOUT THE CITY. THEN EARLY ONE MORNING AS HE PASSED BY THE TUNGABHADRA RIVER —
WHY, IF IT ISN'T THE RAJGURU ABOUT TO GO IN FOR HIS BATH !
HE'S LEFT HIS CLOTHES ON THE BANK!
THE NEXT MOMENT, RAMAN DARTED FORWARD...
...GRABBED THE CLOTHES...
...AND HID THEM BEHIND A ROCK.
SOMETHING TELLS ME, I'LL SOON ENTER THE COURT — GUARDS OR NO GUARDS.

HIS BATH OVER, THE RAJGURU TURNED AND REACHED OUT FOR HIS CLOTHES.
WH-WHERE ARE MY CLOTHES? I'D LEFT THEM RIGHT HERE. WHERE COULD THEY HAVE DISAPPEARED?
RAMAN STEPPED OUT FROM BEHIND THE TREE.
I HAVE THEM. I'LL GIVE THEM TO YOU, ON ONE CONDITION. YOU MUST WALK PAST THE KING'S PALACE CARRYING ME ON YOUR SHOULDERS.
THE RAJGURU HAD TO AGREE.
THE FELLOW MUST BE MAD! BUT I'LL HAVE TO HUMOUR HIM OR CATCH MY DEATH IN THIS ICY WATER.
ALL RIGHT. I'LL CARRY YOU. NOW GIVE ME BACK MY CLOTHES.

AS SOON AS THE PRIEST WAS DRESSED, RAMAN HOISTED HIMSELF ONTO HIS SHOULDERS.
I'M READY. COME LET'S GO. I'D LIKE TO RIDE A FAST HORSE.
THE PRIEST BEGAN WALKING AND THEY SOON APPROACHED THE PALACE.
THE KING WAS OUT ON THE TERRACE, ENJOYING THE MORNING AIR. SUDDENLY—
WH-WHAT'S THAT! NO! IT CANNOT BE! WHICH SELF-RESPECTING MAN WOULD CARRY ANOTHER ON HIS BACK?

CURIOUS, THE KING STARED AT THE FIGURES, WAITING FOR THEM TO COME NEARER.
IT'S MY GURU! SURELY THERE'S SOME MISCHIEF AFOOT!
THE KING! HE'S SEEN US!
HE'S BOUND TO SEND HIS GUARDS OUT. I MUST BE QUICK!
HE SLID DOWN THE RAJGURU'S BACK AND...
...FELL AT HIS FEET.
RESPECTED SIR, I HAVE TRIED YOU ENOUGH. YOU ARE TRULY A HOLY ONE. I SHALL SERVE YOU HUMBLY FOR THE REST OF MY LIFE. LET ME BEGIN BY CARRYING YOU HOME.

BEFORE THE RAJGURU COULD PROTEST, RAMAN HOISTED HIM ON HIS SHOULDERS...
...AND BEGAN WALKING.
MEANWHILE, THE KING HAD SUMMONED HIS GUARDS.
THERE IS A MAN RIDING ON MY EXALTED GURU'S SHOULDERS. I SMELL MISCHIEF. DRAG THE FELLOW DOWN, GIVE HIM A SOUND THRASHING AND LEAD THE GURU TO ME.
THE GUARDS HAD BEEN APPOINTED ONLY THE PREVIOUS EVENING AND THIS WAS THEIR FIRST ASSIGNMENT. THEY WERE EAGER TO MAKE IT A THOROUGH SUCCESS.
THERE THEY ARE!

THEY RUSHED FORWARD...
...DRAGGED THE RAJGURU OFF RAMAN'S BACK...
?
...GAVE HIM A SOUND THRASHING...
...AND ADDRESSED RAMAN IN THE MOST RESPECTFUL TERMS.
O HOLY ONE, THE SCOUNDREL HAS BEEN DEALT WITH. HIS MAJESTY HAS REQUESTED YOU TO PERMIT US TO ESCORT YOU TO HIM.

SOON RAMAN STOOD BEFORE THE KING —
IT'S HAPPENED. I AM IN THE COURT OF THE GREAT KING — AND I MEAN TO STAY HERE FOREVER.

THE KING WAS SURPRISED.
YOU ARE NOT MY GURU. WHO ARE YOU?
I AM RAMAN OF TENALI, YOUR MAJESTY.

BUT ... HOW ... WHERE IS THE GURU?
PARDON ME, YOUR MAJESTY. BUT THE GURU HAS MET WITH THE FATE HE DESERVED.

AND RAMAN TOLD THE KING ALL ABOUT HIS ENCOUNTER WITH THE GURU. THEN—
IF YOUR MAJESTY DEEMS IT FIT TO PUNISH ME, I'LL TAKE THE PUNISHMENT.
BUT THE KING TOOK AN IMMEDIATE LIKING TO THE BOLD, FRANK, FEARLESS RAMAN.
NO, RAMAN. YOU HAVE DONE NO WRONG. MY COURT COULD DO WITH MEN LIKE YOU. FROM THIS VERY MOMENT I APPOINT YOU MY COURT JESTER! BUT...
...IF AT ANY TIME YOU FORGET YOURSELF AND GO TOO FAR WITH YOUR WIT AND YOUR JOKES, YOU SHALL BE HANGED!
THE KING THEN DIPPED INTO HIS CUMMERBUND AND FISHED OUT A BAG OF GOLD COINS.
TAKE THIS. BUY YOURSELF A HOUSE IN VIJAYANAGARA AND SET UP A HOME.
I AM HONOURED, YOUR MAJESTY.

RAMAN COULD HARDLY BELIEVE HIS LUCK.
MY AGED MOTHER AND MY GOOD WIFE WILL BE HAPPY WATCHING ME PROSPER UNDER THE PATRONAGE OF THE GREAT KING. A GREAT DAY INDEED!
THUS DID RAMAN OF TENALI ENTER THE COURT OF THE GREAT KING OF VIJAYANAGARA.

ANXIOUS TO PLEASE THE KING, RAMAN LEFT HOME EARLY EACH MORNING AND RETURNED LATE AT NIGHT. AS HE WAS RETURNING HOME ONE MOONLIT NIGHT—
I HAVE NOT YET FOUND TIME TO WATER MY FIELDS THIS WEEK. TOMORROW I MUST...

SUDDENLY HE STIFFENED. TWO DARK FIGURES, LURKING IN THE SHADOWS, HAD CAUGHT HIS ATTENTION.
THIEVES! THEY DON'T KNOW I'VE SEEN THEM. WELL! WELL! WELL!

HE WALKED STRAIGHT ON TO HIS HOUSE. AS HE ENTERED —
AH! IS THAT YOU? YOUR DINNER IS COLD. I'LL WARM IT UP FOR YOU.
TO HER SURPRISE, RAMAN RAISED HIS VOICE AND ALMOST SHOUTED AT HER.
WE HAD A BUSY DAY AT COURT. THE CITY IS RIDDEN WITH THIEVES AND PEOPLE HAVE BEEN WARNED TO LOCK UP THEIR VALUABLES.
OH DEAR! WHAT SHALL WE DO?
I DON'T EVEN LATCH THE DOOR TILL WE SLEEP.
PUT ALL OUR JEWELLERY, SILVERWARE AND MONEY INTO A TRUNK AND I'LL THROW IT INTO THE WELL. NO THIEF WILL EVER FIND IT.
HA! HA! THAT'S WHAT YOU THINK.

THEN RAMAN STEPPED CLOSER TO HIS WIFE.
THERE ARE TWO THIEVES OUTSIDE. I WANT TO DUPE THEM. FILL THAT TRUNK WITH SOME-THING HEAVY.
RAMAN'S WIFE WAS QUICK TO UNDERSTAND.
THIS GRINDING-STONE SHOULD BE IDEAL.
RAMAN DRAGGED THE TRUNK TO THE WELL...
...AND THREW IT IN, MAKING AS LOUD A SPLASH AS HE COULD.
NOW FOR A GOOD NIGHT'S SLEEP.
A LITTLE LATER, WHEN THE LAMPS WERE BLOWN OUT IN THE HOUSE —
THEY'VE GONE TO BED. IT'S SAFE TO COME OUT. LET'S GET TO WORK.

THEY WENT UP TO THE WELL AND PEEPED IN.
THERE DOESN'T SEEM TO BE MUCH WATER IN THERE.
GOOD! THAT SHOULD MAKE IT EASIER FOR US.
THE FOOLISH THIEVES BEGAN TO DRAIN THE WELL.
THEY WORKED THROUGHOUT THE NIGHT; BUT IN VAIN.
AH! MY BACK! CAN YOU SEE THE TRUNK?
NO. NOT YET. COME ON. WE MUST NOT GIVE UP NOW.
A LITTLE BEFORE DAWN, RAMAN SAW THAT HIS FIELDS HAD HAD ALL THE WATER THEY NEEDED.
IT'S TIME I RELIEVED THE POOR FOOLS.

HE WENT TO THE WELL.
THANK YOU, MY GOOD MEN. YOU HAVE DONE A FINE JOB!

THE STARTLED THIEVES DROPPED THE ROPES...
?!

...AND RAN FOR THEIR LIVES.
HA! HA! HA! WATCH THEM RUN!

* PLAYS BASED ON KRISHNA'S LIFE

MEANWHILE RAMAN CAME TO THE PALACE AND WAS ABOUT TO WALK IN AS USUAL, WHEN—
YOU MAY NOT ENTER. THE KING'S ORDERS. HE IS NOT TO BE DISTURBED.
RAMAN'S CURIOSITY WAS AROUSED.
THERE IS SOMETHING SPECIAL GOING ON AND I HAVE NOT BEEN INVITED. I MUST SEE WHAT IT IS!
HE TURNED TO THE GUARDS.
BUT I MUST SEE THE KING. HE HAS PROMISED ME A REWARD AND HAS ASKED ME TO SEE HIM.
THE REWARD MUST BE A BAG OF GOLD AS USUAL.
HE LOOKED GREEDILY AT RAMAN.
ALL RIGHT! WHAT WILL YOU GIVE ME IF I LET YOU ENTER?
HALF OF WHAT THE KING GIVES ME.

THAT WAS EXACTLY WHAT THE GUARD WANTED TO HEAR.
YOU MAY GO IN, THEN. BUT REMEMBER— HALF OF WHAT YOU GET IS FOR ME.
I'D BETTER RUN IN BEFORE HE CHANGES HIS MIND!
WHEN HE REACHED THE DOOR TO THE AUDIENCE HALL—
STOP! YOU MAY NOT ENTER.
PLEASE DON'T STOP ME. THE KING HAS SENT FOR ME TO COLLECT A REWARD.
A REWARD?
LET ME ENTER AND I'LL GIVE YOU HALF OF WHAT THE KING GIVES ME.
ALL RIGHT. BUT DON'T FORGET... HALF OF WHAT THE KING GIVES YOU...
...IS YOURS!

RAMAN RUSHED INTO THE HALL —
OH! SO THIS WAS IT. I MUST THINK FAST. THE GUARDS ARE WAITING FOR HALF OF WHAT THE KING GIVES ME.
HE RAN UP TO THE PLAYERS...
...AND PICKING UP A STICK...
...BEGAN TO HIT THE CHIEF ACTOR.
AH! OW! MERCY.

RAMAN! STOP IT! HAVE YOU GONE MAD? HOW DARE YOU DISTURB THE PERFORMANCE.
HE TURNED TO HIS ATTENDANTS.
BRING THAT FOOL BEFORE ME.
WHEN RAMAN WAS DRAGGED BEFORE HIM —
YOU HAVE GONE A BIT TOO FAR, RAMAN. YOU SHALL RECEIVE A HUNDRED LASHES FOR THIS IMPUDENCE.
AS AN ATTENDANT RAISED THE WHIP —
PLEASE WAIT, YOUR MAJESTY. I HAVE TWO FRIENDS OUTSIDE WHO WANT TO SHARE THE LASHES.
THE KING WAS ASTONISHED.
WHO ARE THESE FOOLS? HAVE THEM BROUGHT IN.
RAMAN WHISPERED SOMETHING INTO THE ATTENDANT'S EAR.

THE ATTENDANT RETURNED WITH THE TWO GUARDS.
MY GUARDS? WHAT IS THE MEANING OF THIS, RAMAN? DO YOU WANT TO BE BEHEADED?
I AM HONOUR BOUND TO SHARE WITH THEM WHAT YOU WISH TO GIVE ME.
AND HE TOLD THE KING HOW HE HAD GAINED ENTRY INTO THE PALACE AND THE AUDIENCE HALL.
THE KING WAS AT ONCE ANGRY AND AMUSED. ANGRY WITH THE DISHONEST GUARDS AND AMUSED BY RAMAN'S WIT.
HOW DARE YOU ALLOW YOURSELVES TO BE BRIBED INTO DISOBEY-ING MY ORDERS!
HE TURNED TO THE ATTENDANTS.
GIVE THEM FIFTY LASHES EACH AND DISMISS THEM.
THEN HE TURNED TO RAMAN.
I AM GRATEFUL TO YOU, RAMAN, FOR EXPOSING THESE ROGUES. YOU SHALL RECEIVE A BAG OF GOLD FOR YOUR EFFORTS.
THUS DID RAMAN EARN AS USUAL, NOT ONLY THE KING'S FORGIVENESS BUT ALSO A REWARD.

AMAR CHITRA KATHA

Raman the Matchless Wit

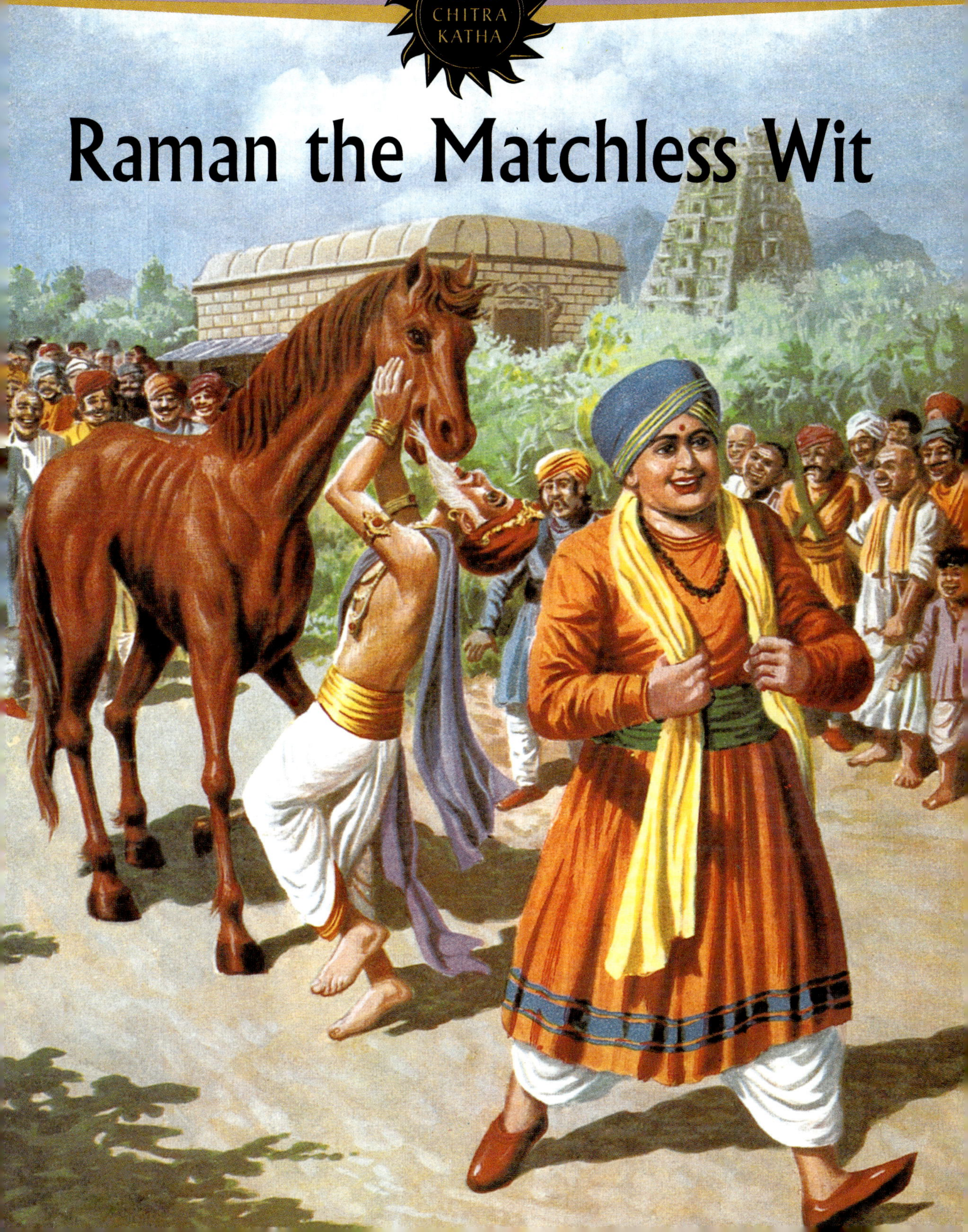

AMAR CHITRA KATHA

Illustrated Classics From India

Raman the Matchless Wit

The triumph of wit over might, of brain over brawn, is a recurring theme in literature. Sometimes, like in the fable of David and Goliath, the gigantic Goliath is defeated with a sling and stone. But more often, like with Tenali Raman, it is done with nimble wit.

Tenali Raman was a Telugu poet and a jester at the court of King Krishnadevaraya of Vijayanagara. He was renowned as the "Birbal of the South" and many stories, which have passed into folklore, are attributed to him. Some of these are obviously invented to show his ready wit. This Amar Chitra Katha narrates amusing incidents from the king's court. As a fitting finale, this volume ends with an anecdote of the inimitable Birbal.

Script: Subba Rao   Illustrations: Ram Waeerkar

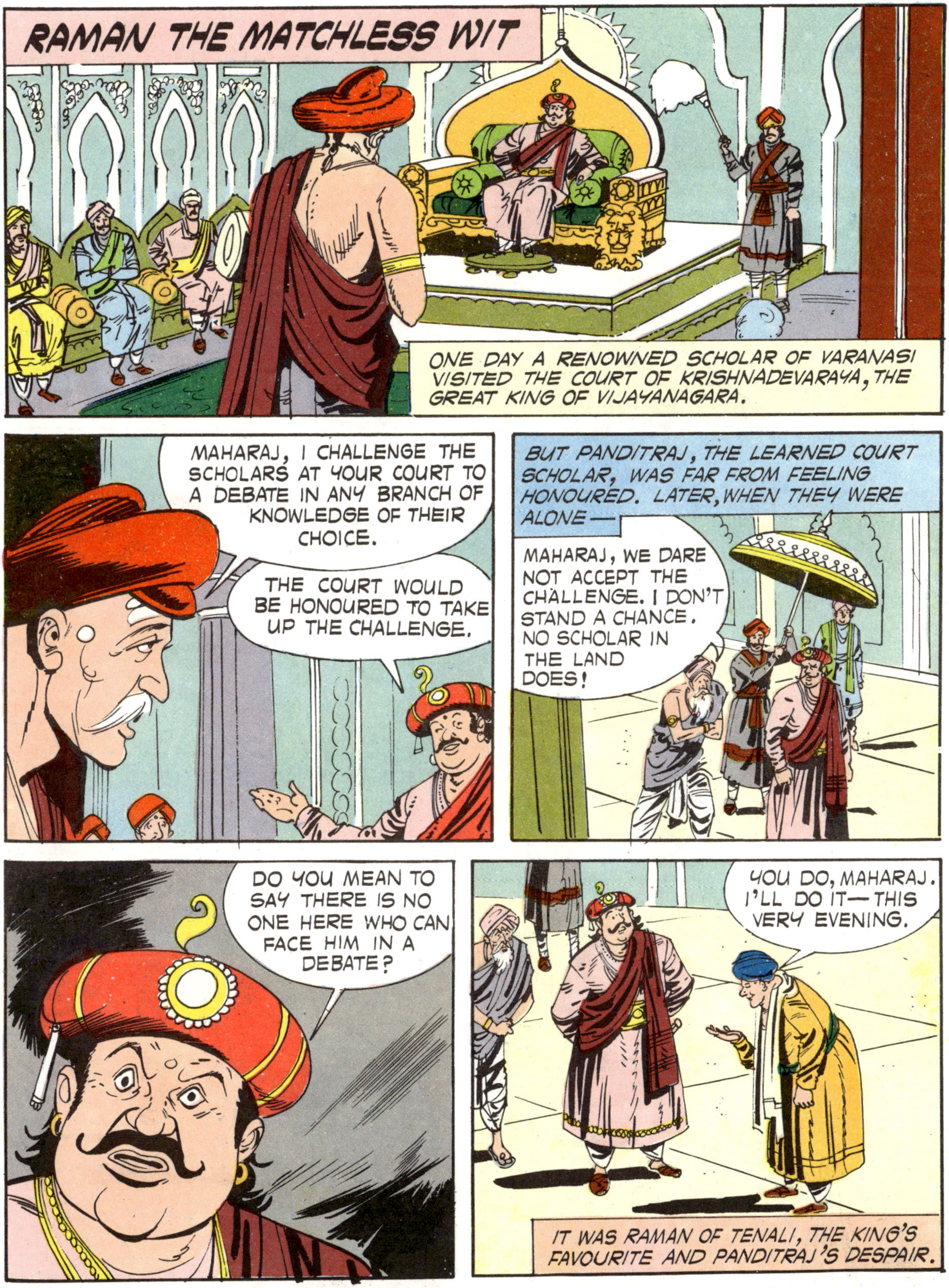
RAMAN THE MATCHLESS WIT
ONE DAY A RENOWNED SCHOLAR OF VARANASI VISITED THE COURT OF KRISHNADEVARAYA, THE GREAT KING OF VIJAYANAGARA.
MAHARAJ, I CHALLENGE THE SCHOLARS AT YOUR COURT TO A DEBATE IN ANY BRANCH OF KNOWLEDGE OF THEIR CHOICE.
THE COURT WOULD BE HONOURED TO TAKE UP THE CHALLENGE.
BUT PANDITRAJ, THE LEARNED COURT SCHOLAR, WAS FAR FROM FEELING HONOURED. LATER, WHEN THEY WERE ALONE —
MAHARAJ, WE DARE NOT ACCEPT THE CHALLENGE. I DON'T STAND A CHANCE. NO SCHOLAR IN THE LAND DOES!
DO YOU MEAN TO SAY THERE IS NO ONE HERE WHO CAN FACE HIM IN A DEBATE?
YOU DO, MAHARAJ. I'LL DO IT — THIS VERY EVENING.
IT WAS RAMAN OF TENALI, THE KING'S FAVOURITE AND PANDITRAJ'S DESPAIR.

THANK YOU, RAMAN. BUT SCHOLARSHIP IS SCHOLARSHIP AND WIT — WIT. I TRUST YOU KNOW WHAT YOU'RE TAKING ON.
I DO, MAHARAJ.
HE DOESN'T! HE'LL SHAME US! MAHARAJ, WE CAN'T . .
PANDITRAJ ! HAVE ARRANGEMENTS MADE FOR THE DEBATE THIS EVENING.
THAT EVENING —
ONE OF OUR MOST LEARNED SCHOLARS, HAS ACCEPTED YOUR CHALLENGE.
HERE HE COMES WITH HIS DISCIPLES.
WELL, RAMAN, MUCH AS I DISLIKE YOU, I'D HATE TO BE IN YOUR SHOES!
PLEASE PLACE THAT BUNDLE OF MANUSCRIPTS HERE.

SHALL WE BEGIN, O LEARNED ONE?
I AM READY. WHICH WORK HAVE YOU CHOSEN TO DEBATE ON?
LET'S BEGIN WITH A SIMPLE ONE.
I EXPECT YOU ARE FAMILIAR WITH THE TILAKASHTHA MAHISHA BANDHANA OF...
TILAKASHTHA...
... MAHISHA BANDHANA... TILAKASHTHA? NO. I AM NOT.
I BEG YOUR PARDON, O PANDIT. I HAVE NEVER COME ACROSS THAT WORK SO...
WHAT! NEVER COME ACROSS IT? THAT'S SURPRISING!

WHY, EVEN COWHERDS IN OUR CITY ARE FAMILIAR WITH IT!
IF MERE COWHERDS IN THIS CITY KNOW WHAT I HAVEN'T EVEN HEARD OF, HOW MUCH MORE INTELLIGENT THIS SCHOLAR MUST BE!
I ACCEPT DEFEAT, O LEARNED ONE. PARDON MY ARROGANCE. THERE IS MUCH I HAVE YET TO LEARN.
AND THE HUMBLE SCHOLAR LEFT THE COURT.
I AM GRATEFUL TO YOU, RAMAN. YOU HAVE SAVED THE REPUTATION OF OUR SCHOLARS.
I'M CURIOUS. WHAT IS THIS GREAT WORK YOU SPOKE ABOUT? I MUST CONFESS THAT I TOO HAVEN'T HEARD OF IT!

RAMAN THEN UN-COVERED HIS BUNDLE.
THESE ARE THE TILAKASHTHAS — STALKS OF THE SESAME PLANT...
...WHICH I HAVE TIED TOGETHER WITH A MAHISHA BANDHANA — THE ROPE WITH WHICH BUFFALOES ARE TETHERED. SIMPLE ISN'T IT?
HA... HA, PANDITRAJ! HE HAS CERTAINLY SHAMED US. BUT NOT IN THE WAY YOU FEARED!
THE ROGUE! HE HAD EVEN ME STUMPED!
PANDITRAJ, WHILE I HOLD YOU IN HIGH ESTEEM FOR YOUR LEARNING, YOU WILL AGREE THAT RAMAN'S WIT IS MATCHLESS!
UNDOUBTEDLY, YOUR MAJESTY.
AS RAMAN WALKED AWAY THOUGH —
TILAKASHTHA MAHISHA BANDHANA, INDEED! I'LL BIDE MY TIME TO HAVE MY REVENGE.

HE DID NOT HAVE TO WAIT LONG.
PANDITRAJ, TOMORROW IS MY MOTHER'S DEATH ANNIVERSARY. I FEEL SAD WHEN I THINK OF HER.
YOU SHOULDN'T, MAHARAJ. THAT WHICH IS BORN HAS TO DIE.
THAT I HAVE ACCEPTED. I FEEL SAD BECAUSE I COULD NOT FULFIL HER LAST WISH.
WHAT WAS THE WISH A MONARCH COULD NOT FULFIL?
HER CRAVING FOR MANGOES. BUT IT WAS NOT THE MANGO SEASON. NO AMOUNT OF GOLD COULD BUY A MANGO.
MANGOES! GOLD!
MAHARAJ, I AM SORRY TO SAY...
YES? SPEAK UP. PLEASE DON'T HESITATE.
YOUR MOTHER DIED WITH AN UN-FULFILLED WISH. HER SOUL WILL REMAIN RESTLESS UNLESS...
UNLESS? UNLESS WHAT?
UNLESS YOU INVITE A FEW VIRTUOUS BRAHMANAS AND...

... PRESENT EACH ONE OF THEM WITH A GOLDEN MANGO.
WHY A FEW? SEND OUT INVITATIONS TO ALL THE BRAHMANAS
HERE'S WHERE I'LL HAVE MY REVENGE. I WON'T SEND AN INVITATION TO THAT ROGUE.
RAMAN HOWEVER, COULD NOT RESIST WATCHING THE WHOLE SHOW.
SO, THE BRAHMANAS WILL OBLIGE THE KING AND ACCEPT THE GOLDEN MANGOES FOR THE SAKE OF THE LATE QUEEN MOTHER'S SOUL! WELL, WELL.
AFTER THE BRAHMANAS WERE FED AND PRESENTED WITH THE GOLDEN MANGOES—
I AM GRATEFUL TO YOU FOR HAVING ACCEPTED MY INVITATION.
MAY GOD BLESS YOU. YOU NEED NO LONGER FEEL SAD WHEN YOU THINK OF YOUR MOTHER. HER SOUL IS NOW AT PEACE.

WHEN THE BRAHMANAS CAME OUT OF THE PALACE —
LEARNED ONES, TODAY IS MY MOTHER'S DEATH ANNIVERSARY, TOO. AND SHE TOO DIED WITH AN UNFULFILLED WISH.
AS YOU KNOW, HER SOUL WILL BE RESTLESS TILL A FEW VIRTUOUS BRAHMANAS AGREE TO...
WE UNDERSTAND, RAMAN. WE'LL COME.
I AM HONOURED!
THIS WAY, MY FRIENDS.
I WONDER WHAT GIFTS RAMAN IS GOING TO OFFER US.
RAMAN TOOK THEM TO THE BACKYARD OF HIS HOUSE.
COME, LET ME WASH YOUR FEET BEFORE...
WHAT ARE THEY DOING?

WHY ARE THOSE RODS BEING HEATED?
MY MOTHER DIED OF RHEUMATISM. HER LAST WISH WAS TO HAVE HER LEGS BRANDED.
BUT...
BEFORE I COULD GET THE IRONS READY, SHE DIED.
HER SOUL WILL KNOW NO PEACE UNTIL...
...I BRAND THE LEGS OF LEARNED AND DESERVING BRAHMANAS. SHALL WE BEGIN?
YOU CAN'T BE SERIOUS!
YOU ARE MAD!
I AM HURT. DON'T YOU WANT MY MOTHER'S SOUL TO FIND PEACE. YOU DID HELP THE EMPEROR, SO I...
...

YES, RAMAN, BUT THAT WAS DIFFERENT. HERE, YOU CAN KEEP THESE. BUT DO TRY TO UNDERSTAND.
WHAT ABOUT...
...MY MOTHER'S LAST WISH?
LOOK AT THEM SCURRYING AWAY! LIKE A PACK OF RATS!
WHAT A PITY WE HAD TO PART WITH OUR MANGOES!
LET'S COMPLAIN TO THE KING AND HAVE RAMAN PUNISHED!
BUT WHEN THE KING HEARD THE STORY—
THANK YOU, RAMAN, FOR SHOWING ME WHAT A GULLIBLE FOOL I WAS!

WHAT A FOOL! HA! HA! HO! HA!
THIS IS NO LAUGHING MATTER, MAHARAJ. MEN OF LEARNING HAVE BEEN INSULTED.
AH! YES! THAT'S TRUE! I HADN'T LOOKED AT IT THAT WAY!
RAMAN SHOULD BE PUNISHED. WHAT DO YOU SUGGEST?
LET HIM PAY FOR IT WITH HIS HEAD!
WELL! I'LL HUMOUR HIM, FOR I CAN TRUST RAMAN TO TAKE CARE OF HIMSELF.
GONG
TAKE RAMAN TO THE BANK OF THE TUNGABHADRA AND CUT OFF HIS HEAD WITH ONE SWEEP OF YOUR SWORD.
RID OF HIM AT LAST!

WITH ONE SWEEP OF YOUR SWORD, DID YOU SAY? WELL IF THAT'S MY FATE, I GUESS I'LL HAVE TO ACCEPT IT LIKE A MAN.
ON THE BANK OF, THE TUNGABHADRA —
YOU ARE ABOUT TO DIE, RAMAN. IF YOU TELL US YOUR LAST WISH...
... WE'LL TRY AND FULFIL IT.
I WANT YOU TO PRAY WITH ME — FOR ME. PLEASE SAY YOU WILL.
OF COURSE, WE WILL, RAMAN.
I WANT YOU TO CUT OFF MY NECK THE MOMENT I CALL OUT TO MOTHER KALI.
WE'LL SEE THAT WE DO, RAMAN.
JUST A MINUTE. WHO WILL CUT OFF HIS HEAD? YOU OR I?
BOTH OF YOU! AT THE SAME TIME.

BOTH OF US?
YES, IF YOU MISS, YOUR FRIEND WILL GET ME. IF HE MISSES, YOU'LL GET ME.
WHAT IS IMPORTANT IS THAT I MUST DIE WITH THE NAME OF MOTHER KALI ON MY LIPS.
WE WON'T FAIL YOU, RAMAN. SHALL WE GET READY?
JAI KALI!

WH - WHERE IS HE?
I'D LIKE TO KNOW.
RIGHT HERE, FRIENDS.
STAND UP, YOU ROGUE! WE'LL KILL YOU WITHOUT FAIL THIS TIME.
NOW, NOW! REMEMBER THE KING'S ORDERS? "CUT OFF HIS HEAD WITH ONE SWEEP OF YOUR SWORD!"
YOU'LL HAVE TO GET HIS PERMISSION FOR A SECOND TRY.
ALL RIGHT! ALL RIGHT! LET'S GO TO THE KING THEN.
SO RAMAN WAS TAKEN TO THE KING.
WHAT ARE YOU DOING HERE?
WHY HAVEN'T YOU EXECUTED HIM?

WHEN THE KING WAS TOLD WHY—
WELL PANDITRAJ... WHAT DO YOU SUGGEST NOW?
LET RAMAN BE BURIED UP TO HIS NECK AND BE TRAMPLED TO DEATH BY AN ELEPHANT.
GO! DO AS HE SAYS!
AM I GOING TO LOSE YOU, RAMAN? I CAN'T SEE HOW YOU'LL GET OUT OF THIS ONE.
THE GUARDS TOOK RAMAN TO THE OUTSKIRTS OF THE CITY AND BEGAN TO DIG THE GROUND.
AT LAST THE PIT WAS READY.
GET IN THERE! AND NONE OF YOUR TRICKS THIS TIME.
MY FRIENDS, I KNOW WHEN TO ACCEPT DEFEAT.

RAMAN ENTERED THE PIT AND THE GUARDS SEALED HIM IN WITH MUD.
NOW, LET'S HAVE LUNCH AND COME BACK WITH THE ELEPHANT.
AREN'T ONE OF YOU GOING TO STAY BACK AND STAND GUARD?
THERE'S NO NEED TO. YOU CAN'T RUN AWAY.
I WON'T. BUT I MAY BE RUN OVER BY A CHARIOT OR...
HE! HE! HE! HE'S WORRIED ABOUT BEING RUN OVER!
WE WILL SOON PUT AN END TO ALL YOUR WORRIES.
MOTHER KALI, ONLY YOU CAN SAVE ME NOW. IF ONLY SOME ONE WOULD PASS THIS WAY....

AS IF IN ANSWER TO HIS PRAYER, A WASHERMAN CAME BY.
AM I SEEING THINGS? OR IS THAT THE HEAD OF A MAN?
IT IS! HE MUST BE A YOGI.
THE WASHERMAN WALKED UP TO RAMAN —
GURU MAHARAJ, I SEEK YOUR BLESSINGS.
THANK YOU, O GODDESS!
MY FRIEND, WHO AM I TO BLESS YOU? I AM AN ORDINARY WASHERMAN LIKE YOU.
A WASHERMAN! THEN WHY HAVE YOU BURIED YOURSELF LIKE THIS?
I AM UNDER TREATMENT. I AM A HUNCHBACK.
BUT SURELY, THERE'S NO REMEDY FOR THAT!
THERE IS, MY FRIEND — A SIMPLE ONE. BURY YOURSELF LIKE THIS FOR AN HOUR; AND YOU WILL WALK ERECT.
I DON'T BELIEVE YOU.

WHY DON'T YOU HELP ME GET OUT OF THIS PIT AND SEE FOR YOURSELF.
THE WASHERMAN BEGAN TO DIG UP THE SOIL AROUND RAMAN.
WHEN RAMAN CAME OUT OF THE PIT—
I CAN'T BELIEVE IT!
AMAZING, ISN'T IT? I TOO CARRIED HEAVY LOADS. I TOO HAD BECOME DEFORMED. I TOO USED TO STOOP AS YOU DO. THEN A LEARNED PHYSICIAN SUGGESTED THIS TREATMENT.
MY GOOD FRIEND, CAN I TRY IT TOO?
WHY NOT? ALL YOU HAVE TO DO IS STAND IN A PIT WITH MUD PACKED AROUND YOU.
THEN I'LL STAND IN THIS VERY PIT.

WILL YOU FILL IN THE MUD?
CERTAINLY. IT WOULD BE A PLEASURE TO BE OF HELP TO YOU.
REMEMBER, YOU WILL HAVE TO REMAIN IN THE PIT FOR AT LEAST AN HOUR.
OH DEAR! I HAVE TO DELIVER THOSE CLOTHES TO THE PALACE.
DON'T WORRY. I'LL DELIVER THEM FOR YOU.
WHAT A GOOD MAN YOU ARE, MY FRIEND! I DON'T KNOW HOW TO THANK YOU!

ON HIS WAY TO THE PALACE, RAMAN PASSED THE GUARDS WHO WERE RETURNING WITH THE ELEPHANT.
HURRY UP, THE QUEEN IS WAITING FOR THE CLOTHES.
THANK GOD! THEY HAVEN'T RECOGNISED ME!
I AM WALKING AS FAST AS I CAN, SIR.
LATER, AT THE PIT—
AN ELEPHANT! I HOPE THE MAHOUT CAN SEE ME.
THERE HE IS. SEE THAT THE ELEPHANT DOES NOT MISS HIM.
HE WON'T!
MY GOD! HE'S HEADING FOR ME.

HELP! HELP!
HEY! THAT ISN'T RAMAN. I KNOW HIS VOICE.
THE GUARDS RAN FORWARD —
HELP! HELP!
WHO ARE YOU? WHAT ARE YOU DOING HERE?
I AM UNDER TREATMENT. A LEARNED PHYSICIAN SUGGESTED IT TO MY FRIEND. ALL ONE HAS TO DO IS....
YES, YES. BUT WHERE IS RAMAN?
YOU MEAN, THE KIND YOUNG WASHERMAN WHO LET ME USE THIS PIT? HE HAS TAKEN THE LAUNDRY TO THE PALACE FOR ME.
YOU MEAN... NO! THE SCOUNDREL HAS TRICKED US AGAIN!
MY FRIEND? A SCOUNDREL? IMPOSSIBLE. HE IS A GOOD MAN...

YOU FOOL! HE IS A SCOUNDREL! HE WAS TO BE TRAMPLED TO DEATH BY THIS ELEPHANT.
I DON'T UNDERSTAND.
THEN THE GUARDS HELPED THE POOR WASHERMAN TO COME OUT OF THE PIT.
MY BACK! IT'S STILL BENT!
IT WILL BE BROKEN, IF THE EMPEROR HEARS THAT YOU HELPED RAMAN ESCAPE.
HOWEVER, WHEN THE KING DID HEAR ABOUT IT—
HA! HA! WASN'T THAT CLEVER OF HIM, PANDITRAJ?
BUT MAHARAJ...
PANDITRAJ, I THINK IT'S GOD'S WILL THAT RAMAN SHOULD LIVE TO MAKE PEOPLE LAUGH.
JUST THEN A MERCHANT FROM ARABIA ENTERED THE COURT.
YOUR MAJESTY, I HAVE SOME STRONG, SWIFT-FOOTED, ARABIAN HORSES FOR SALE. THE FINEST HORSES IN THE WORLD!

YOU WILL NEVER FIND BETTER HORSES THAN THOSE I'VE BROUGHT.
THEN SEND THE LOT TO ME.
THE KING ALLOTTED A HORSE TO EACH COURTIER.
I WANT YOU TO TAKE GOOD CARE OF YOUR HORSES AND HAVE THEM TRAINED. ONE MONTH FROM TODAY, A RACE WILL BE HELD. THE MASTER OF THE WINNER WILL BE HANDSOMELY REWARDED.
AFTER THE COURTIERS HAD LED AWAY THEIR HORSES —
MAHARAJ, WHY HAVEN'T I BEEN ALLOTTED ONE?
WHAT WOULD A FOOL KNOW ABOUT TRAINING HORSES! THAT'S WHY!
PANDITRAJ IS RIGHT, RAMAN. I DON'T THINK YOU WILL BE ABLE TO TRAIN A HORSE.

PLEASE, LET ME TRY, MAHARAJ. I AM CONFIDENT I'LL SUCCEED. PLEASE GIVE ME A CHANCE.
HM— M—M. ALL RIGHT. PANDITRAJ, LET RAMAN BE GIVEN A HORSE TOO.
RAMAN LED THE HORSE TO HIS HOUSE...
...AND BUILT A STABLE FOR IT.
IT WAS A STRANGE STABLE, WALLED IN ON ALL SIDES WITH JUST ONE WEE WINDOW...
...THROUGH WHICH RAMAN FED IT ITS DAILY RATION OF HAY.

A MONTH LATER, THE COURTIERS CAME WITH THEIR HORSES, ALL SET FOR THE RACE.
ARE ALL THE HORSES HERE?
ALL BUT RAMAN'S, MAHARAJ. I KNEW HE...
RAMAN, WHERE IS THE HORSE?
MAHARAJ, IT'S SUCH A FIERCE BEAST, THAT I DARE NOT GO NEAR IT.
I DON'T BELIEVE HIM, MAHARAJ. HE'S ASHAMED OF HIS HORSE. THAT'S WHY HE HASN'T BROUGHT IT.
IS THAT SO?
MAHARAJ, I DON'T LIE. PLEASE BELIEVE ME. I DARE NOT GO NEAR IT.
THAT'S JUST AN EXCUSE, MAHARAJ. FOR ALL WE KNOW HE MIGHT HAVE SOLD IT.
MAHARAJ, I AM HURT. IF PANDITRAJ DOES NOT BELIEVE ME, LET HIM COME AND SEE FOR HIMSELF.
GO, PANDITRAJ, AND BRING THE HORSE HERE.

TO BE SURE I WILL, MAHARAJ. I'LL PERSONALLY LEAD IT HERE. IF IT'S STILL THERE!
PANDITRAJ WENT WITH RAMAN.
WHERE IS IT?
THERE! IN THAT STABLE I MADE SPECIALLY FOR IT.
YOU FOOL, DO YOU CALL THAT A STABLE?
PANDITRAJ, PLEASE DON'T BE ANGRY. I AM NOT A LEARNED MAN. I DON'T KNOW BETTER.
LET ME SEE THE HORSE.
THIS WAY. YOU CAN SEE IT THROUGH THIS WINDOW. BUT TAKE CARE.
THE MOMENT PANDITRAJ PUT HIS HEAD INTO THE WINDOW...
...THE STARVING ANIMAL GRABBED HIS BEARD, MISTAKING IT FOR HAY!

OW-W-W!
RAMAN! HELP ME!
I DAREN'T. AND YOU CAN'T SAY I DIDN'T WARN YOU.
ATTRACTED BY THE COMMOTION, A CROWD SOON COLLECTED.
WE'LL HAVE TO BREAK THAT WALL DOWN. THERE'S NO ALTERNATIVE.
THEN LET'S BREAK IT.
AT LAST THE WALLS WERE HACKED DOWN. BUT—
THE WRETCHED BEAST WON'T LET GO! WHAT SHALL I DO?

PANDITRAJ, IT'S THE KING'S HORSE. ONLY HE CAN DECIDE WHAT'S TO BE DONE.
AND YOU'VE PROMISED THAT YOU WOULD PERSONALLY LEAD IT TO THE PALACE.
BUT NOT BY MY BEARD!
THERE IS NO ALTERNATIVE. LET'S GO.
ISN'T THAT PANDITRAJ?
WHAT A CRUEL FELLOW! WHAT'S HE TRYING TO DO TO THE POOR HORSE?
AT LAST THE PROCESSION REACHED THE PALACE GROUNDS.
MAHARAJ, MY HORSE.
HA! HA! HA!
MAHARAJ, PLEASE RELEASE ME FROM THE JAWS OF THIS VICIOUS CREATURE.

PANDITRAJ, NOW DO YOU BELIEVE ME?
I DO! I DO!
RAMAN! ENOUGH OF YOUR PRANKS!
I BEG YOUR PARDON, MAHARAJ.
YOU THERE! GET ME A BUNDLE OF HAY.
WHEN THE HAY WAS BROUGHT—
CLEVER RAMAN HAS SCORED AGAIN! YET I MUST PACIFY PANDITRAJ.
RAMAN, YOU HAVE GONE TOO FAR THIS TIME. DON'T EVER SHOW ME YOUR FACE AGAIN.
AS YOU COMMAND, MAHARAJ.

HM-M-M! I'VE SENT HIM AWAY. BUT I'M GOING TO MISS HIM.
THE NEXT MORNING, AS SOON AS THE KING OPENED HIS EYES, HE WAS GREETED BY A STRANGE FIGURE.
WHO ARE YOU?
RAMAN, MAHARAJ.
RAMAN? DIDN'T I ASK YOU NOT TO SHOW YOUR FACE TO ME?
THAT'S WHY I'VE COVERED IT, MAHARAJ.
THE KING COULD NOT HELP LAUGHING.
HA! HA! RAMAN, IT'S IMPOSSIBLE TO BE ANGRY WITH YOU.
THE KING HIMSELF REMOVED THE POT THAT COVERED RAMAN'S FACE.
THE GODS THEMSELVES CANNOT OUTWIT YOU, RAMAN. MAY YOU LIVE LONG!

BIRBAL'S DARK SECRET
ONE DAY ON ARRIVING AT COURT, BIRBAL WAS SURPRISED.
HEE HEE!
HA HA!
GIGGLE GIGGLE.
WHAT'S SO FUNNY? WHY IS EVERY-ONE IN A MERRY MOOD?
HA! HA! WE WERE DISCUSSING THE COLOUR OF OUR SKINS.
IT IS SO ODD. HEE HEE!
MOST OF US ARE SO FAIR.
BUT YOU ARE QUITE DARK!
BIRBAL WAS QUICK TO RETORT.
BUT DON'T YOU KNOW THE SECRET OF MY DARK SKIN AND PLAIN LOOKS?
SECRET?
WHEN GOD CREATED THE EARTH WITH ALL ITS FLORA AND FAUNA HE WAS STILL NOT SATISFIED. THEN HE SET ABOUT TO MAKE HIS BEST CREATURE — MAN!

HE WAS HAPPY WITH THE RESULTS. HE THEN DECIDED TO BESTOW HIS SPECIAL GIFTS ON MAN.
"BEAUTY, INTELLECT, STRENGTH AND WEALTH, THESE WERE THE GIFTS HE DECIDED TO BESTOW ON THE MEN HE CREATED."
I GIVE YOU FIVE MINUTES. COLLECT WHATEVER YOU CAN OUT OF THESE BOUNTIES.
I WAS SO BUSY COLLECTING INTELLECT THAT I HAD NO TIME LEFT FOR THE OTHER GIFTS.
BUT ALL OF YOU WERE LURED BY BEAUTY AND WEALTH AND HAD NO TIME LEFT TO GATHER INTELLECT.
YOU CAN SEE THE RESULTS YOURSELF.
THE ANSWER SILENCED THE COURTIERS.
BUT THE EMPEROR WAS AMUSED.
HA! HA! WELL SAID, BIRBAL.

AMAR CHITRA KATHA

Birbal the Just

Illustrated Classics From India

Birbal The Just

Birbal had the rare distinction of achieving immense popularity during his lifetime, next only to that of Akbar. His sharp intellect saw him rise to a prominent position as a minister in the court of Akbar. He was a fair administrator, a brave soldier and, perhaps what pleased Akbar the most, a good jester. The wit and wisdom of Birbal had endeared him not only to Akbar, but also to a vast majority of the subjects of the Mughal Empire. His phenomenal success made many courtiers jealous and, if popular accounts are to be believed, they were ever busy plotting against him.

This Amar Chitra Katha narrates some incidents of Birbal's sense of justice and fair play. He solved the commoner's problems using wisdom and ingenuity at times, and wile and cunning at others. Perhaps one of the most famous of Birbal's exploits is that described in 'Birbal's Khichdi'.

The fact that Birbal was also a good poet is little known. He wrote under the pen name 'Brahma' and a collection of his poems is preserved in the Bharatpur Museum. Though popularly known as Birbal, his real name was Maheshdas. It is believed that he belonged to a poor Brahmin family of Trivikrampur (now known as Tikawanpur), on the banks of River Yamuna.

According to legend, even his death, while leading a large military expedition to Afghanistan, was a result of treachery. Though he was killed in battle, the expedition was successful and managed to subdue the turbulent province. Akbar was so moved when he heard of Birbal's death that he burst forth into a couplet and lamented, "Birbal, you never hurt the helpless. You always gave them whatever you had. I am helpless now and yet you have left nothing for me." Akbar found in Birbal a true friend and sympathiser.

Script: Anant Pai Illustrations: A.S. Chitrak
Cover: A.S. Chitrak

BIRBAL, THE JUST

BIRBAL WAS A MINISTER AT THE COURT OF THE GREAT MUGHAL EMPEROR, AKBAR. HE WAS OFTEN CALLED UPON TO DISPENSE JUSTICE.

ONCE, A RICH MERCHANT OF DELHI CAME TO HIM WITH A COMPLAINT.
HUZUR, A BAG CONTAINING ALL MY MONEY HAS BEEN STOLEN. PLEASE HELP ME FIND THE THIEF.
WHOM DO YOU SUSPECT?
I THINK ONE OF MY SERVANTS COULD BE THE THIEF. BUT WITHOUT BEING CERTAIN, HOW CAN I TAKE ANY ACTION?
BIRBAL THOUGHT FOR A WHILE. THEN-
IF THE THIEF IS ONE OF YOUR SERVANTS, WE CAN EASILY FIND HIM OUT.
THE NEXT DAY THE MERCHANT TOOK HIS SEVEN SERVANTS WITH HIM TO BIRBAL'S HOUSE.
A MAGICIAN HAS GIVEN ME THESE STICKS; THEY HELP TO DETECT THIEVES.

EACH OF THE SERVANTS WAS GIVEN A STICK.
IF ANY ONE OF THESE STICKS IS TOUCHED BY A THIEF IT WILL GROW BY EXACTLY AN INCH, OVERNIGHT.
YOU WILL ALL BE GIVEN SEPARATE ROOMS TO STAY IN. WHEN WE MEET TOMORROW, WE WILL KNOW WHO THE THIEF IS.
THE SERVANTS WERE SHOWN THEIR ROOMS.
NEXT MORNING, THE SERVANTS WERE BROUGHT BEFORE BIRBAL.
NOW MEASURE THE STICKS ONE BY ONE.

HUZUR, THIS STICK IS SHORTER BY ONE INCH.
THAT MAN IS THE THIEF! ARREST HIM!
BUT HUZUR, YOU SAID YESTERDAY THAT THE STICK WOULD GROW BY AN INCH.
BECAUSE I SAID THAT, THE REAL THIEF CUT HIS STICK SHORT BY ONE INCH... EXACTLY WHAT I HAD EXPECTED HIM TO DO.
THE THIEF WAS PUT IN JAIL, AND THE MERCHANT WAS HAPPY THAT JUSTICE HAD BEEN RENDERED.

THE OILMAN AND THE BUTCHER
ONCE, AN OILMAN AND A BUTCHER CAME TO BIRBAL WITH A COMPLAINT.

BIRBAL FIRST HEARD THE BUTCHER.
HUZUR, I WAS BUSY SELLING MEAT WHEN THIS OILMAN ENTERED MY SHOP.

"...HE WANTED TO SELL OIL TO ME ...
WAIT HERE, WHILE I FETCH A VESSEL FOR THE OIL.

"WHEN I WENT IN, HE QUIETLY PICKED UP MY MONEY BAG...
"... AND RAN AWAY WITH IT."
I RAN AFTER HIM AND RETRIEVED MY BAG, BUT HE STILL CLAIMS THAT IT IS HIS.
HUZUR, I DID ENTER HIS SHOP. BUT THE REST OF HIS STORY IS NOT TRUE. IT WAS LIKE THIS.

"HE PAID FOR THE OIL HE HAD BOUGHT...
"...WHEN I OPENED MY MONEY BAG TO PUT IN THE MONEY I HAD RECEIVED FROM HIM...
SO MUCH MONEY.
"HE BECAME GREEDY AND SEIZED MY MONEY BAG...
"...I RAN AFTER HIM AND CAUGHT UP WITH HIM. BUT HE REFUSED TO GIVE MY MONEY BACK TO ME."

THE OFFICERS WERE BAFFLED.
HOW CAN BIRBAL GIVE THE VERDICT IN A CASE LIKE THIS?
GO, AND GET A TUB OF HOT WATER.
PUT THE MONEY BAG IN THE TUB.
NOW LET ME INSPECT THE WATER.
HMM...THERE ARE DROPS OF OIL IN THE WATER. THE DROPS COME FROM THE MONEY BAG.
SUCH AN OILY MONEY BAG COULD ONLY BELONG TO AN OILMAN. SEIZE THE BUTCHER AND SEND HIM TO PRISON.

THE RELIABLE WITNESS
AN OLD MAN WENT ON A PILGRIMAGE AFTER GIVING A BAG CONTAINING A THOUSAND GOLD COINS TO HIS FRIEND FOR SAFE-KEEPING.
WHEN HE RETURNED—
FRIEND, I AM BACK HOME. PLEASE RETURN MY BAG.
WHAT BAG ARE YOU TALKING ABOUT? YOU NEVER GAVE ME ANY.
THE BAG CONTAINED ALL MY SAVINGS. PLEASE DON'T JOKE WITH ME. GIVE ME MY BAG.
WHAT BAG ARE YOU TALKING ABOUT? YOU NEVER GAVE ME ANY, YOU OLD FOOL.

SINCE NO ONE COULD RESOLVE THE DISPUTE, THE TWO MEN WERE BROUGHT BEFORE BIRBAL.
WHERE EXACTLY DID YOU HAND OVER THE BAG OF MONEY TO YOUR FRIEND?
UNDER A MANGO TREE IN A MANGO GROVE.
IT IS A LIE, HUZUR.
UNDER A MANGO TREE? YOU NEVER TOLD ME THIS. THAT TREE CAN BE BROUGHT HERE AS A WITNESS.
!!!
GO IMMEDIATELY TO THE TREE, AND ORDER IT TO COME HERE.
?
!?

THE OLD MAN WAS PERPLEXED.
HOW CAN A TREE COME HERE AS A WITNESS? BUT IF I DON'T GO, BIRBAL WILL BE ANGRY.
SO HE LEFT FOR THE GROVE.
MEANWHILE, IN BIRBAL'S PALACE —
WE HAVE BEEN WAITING FOR THE OLD MAN FOR MORE THAN AN HOUR.
BE PATIENT. HE WILL SOON BE BACK.
HOW CAN THE OLD MAN BE BACK SOON? HE COULD NOT EVEN HAVE REACHED THE PLACE.
IS THE MANGO GROVE FAR FROM HERE?
IT IS MORE THAN THREE MILES AWAY.

WELL, WE SHALL WAIT TILL HE RETURNS.
HOURS LATER, THE OLD MAN RETURNED.
WHAT HAPPENED?
HUZUR, I REPEATED YOUR ORDER THRICE TO THE TREE. BUT IT DID NOT MOVE.
DON'T WORRY. THAT MANGO TREE HAS ALREADY BORNE WITNESS.
BIRBAL NOW TURNED TO THE OLD MAN'S FRIEND–
YOU ARE A LIAR! THE OLD MAN DID GIVE THE MONEY BAG TO YOU. HOW ELSE COULD YOU KNOW WHICH GROVE HE WAS GOING TO AND HOW FAR AWAY IT WAS?

THE MASTER AND HIS SLAVE
ONE DAY, THE KOTWAL OF DELHI BROUGHT TWO MEN TO AKBAR'S COURT
JAHANPANAH, THE KAZI COULD NOT RESOLVE THE DISPUTE BETWEEN THESE TWO MEN. SO I HAVE BROUGHT THEM HERE.
THE EMPEROR RECOGNISED ONE OF THE MEN.
SHER ALI, WHAT BRINGS YOU HERE?
JAHANPANAH! AS YOU ARE AWARE, I AM A TRADER AND I HAVE BEEN IN DELHI FOR MORE THAN FIVE YEARS.

BEFORE I CAME TO DELHI, I WAS IN AFGHANISTAN. THIS MAN WAS MY SLAVE. TODAY WHEN I SAW HIM IN DELHI, I CAUGHT HOLD OF HIM.
JAHANPANAH! THE MAN IS A LIAR. HIS NAME IS NOT SHER ALI BUT NASIBA. HE WAS MY SLAVE. HE RAN AWAY WITH MY MONEY AND OTHER VALUABLES. AFTER SEVEN YEARS OF SEARCHING, I FOUND HIM TODAY IN DELHI.

JAHANPANAH, HE IS NASIBA AND IS MY SLAVE. I CAN BRING WITNESSES WHO WILL VOUCH THAT I AM SHER ALI.
VERY LIKELY. FROM THE DAY YOU RAN AWAY FROM ME WITH MY MONEY AND VALUABLES...

... YOU MUST HAVE BEEN MASQUERADING AS SHER ALI, NASIBA.
BE QUIET. BIRBAL WILL DECIDE YOUR CASE.
NASIBA? HOW DARE YOU CALL ME NASIBA!
I WILL CLOSE MY EYES AND MEDITATE. I WILL SOON KNOW WHO THE LIAR IS. MEANWHILE, BOTH OF YOU MUST LIE FLAT ON YOUR STOMACH ON THE FLOOR.
BIRBAL SUDDENLY OPENED HIS EYES.
I KNOW THE TRUTH NOW. CALL IN THE EXECUTIONER.

WHEN THE EXECUTIONER CAME WITH HIS AXE–
CHOP OFF THE SLAVE'S HEAD.
NOW THE GUILTY ONE IS BOUND TO REACT.
AS THE EXECUTIONER RAISED HIS AXE...
...THE DELHI MERCHANT SPRANG TO HIS FEET.
HUZUR, SPARE MY LIFE.
ALL THE PROPERTY OF THE MAN, POSING AS SHER ALI WAS RESTORED TO THE REAL OWNER, AND NASIBA WAS IMPRISONED.

* A DISH PREPARED OUT OF RICE AND LENTILS.

JAHANPANAH! NO ONE WHO SPENDS THE WHOLE NIGHT IN THIS ICE-COLD WATER CAN SURVIVE. LET THE CONDITIONS BE SOMEWHAT EASIER.
NO. I WILL NOT CHANGE THE CONDITIONS.
A POOR BRAHMAN, WHO HAD HEARD THE EMPEROR, DEBATED WITH HIMSELF.
IF I TRY, I MIGHT DIE. ON THE OTHER HAND, IF I SURVIVE TILL MORNING, MY FAMILY WILL GET 50,000 GOLD COINS.
HE STEPPED FORWARD.
JAHANPANAH, I AM PREPARED TO ACCEPT YOUR CHALLENGE.
GOOD! I WILL LEAVE TWO GUARDS AS WITNESSES.

THE POOR BRAHMAN SPENT THE WHOLE NIGHT IN THE COLD LAKE.
AT SUNRISE, HE CAME OUT OF THE WATER.
GUARDS! PLEASE TAKE ME TO THE EMPEROR.
THE GUARDS BROUGHT HIM TO THE COURT.
JAHANPANAH, I HAVE SPENT THE WHOLE NIGHT IN THE LAKE.
YES, JAHANPANAH! WHAT THE BRAHMAN SAYS IS TRUE.

WELL THEN, LET HIM BE GIVEN 50,000 GOLD COINS, AS PROMISED BY ME.

BUT A JEALOUS COURTIER INTERVENED.
TELL ME, O BRAHMAN, HOW DID YOU SPEND THE NIGHT?
AS I HAVE ALREADY SAID – I SPENT THE NIGHT IN THE WATER.

WERE YOU LOOKING AT ANYTHING?
WELL, I SPENT PART OF THE TIME LOOKING AT THE PALACE LIGHTS.

IN THAT CASE, YOU DID DERIVE WARMTH FROM THE PALACE LIGHTS. YOU DIDN'T FULFIL THE CONDITIONS. YOU DO NOT DESERVE THE REWARD.
THIS WAS UNFAIR, BUT THE EMPEROR DID NOT UTTER A WORD AS THE BRAHMAN LOOKED TO HIM FOR JUSTICE.
BIRBAL, HOWEVER, MADE A VOW.
I WILL SEE TO IT THAT THE POOR MAN GETS HIS DUE.
A FEW DAYS LATER, BIRBAL INVITED AKBAR AND A FEW COURTIERS TO DINNER.

AFTER A COUPLE OF HOURS, WHEN THE EMPEROR SAW THAT THERE WAS NO SIGN OF FOOD–
BIRBAL, WE ARE HUNGRY. WHY DO YOU KEEP US WAITING?
THE KHICHDI IS TAKING A LONG TIME TO COOK.
THREE HOURS LATER –
HOW LONG DO YOU THINK IT WILL BE BEFORE YOUR KHICHDI IS READY?
LET'S GO AND SEE.
BIRBAL LED THE EMPEROR AND THE COURTIERS TO HIS BACKYARD.
JAHANPANAH! THAT IS THE POT IN WHICH THE KHICHDI IS BEING COOKED.

BAH! WHAT NONSENSE! HOW CAN THE HEAT REACH THE POT?
WHY NOT? IF A POOR MAN CAN RECEIVE WARMTH BY JUST LOOKING AT THE PALACE LIGHTS, MANY MILES AWAY, WHY CAN'T THE POT RECEIVE WARMTH FROM A FIRE BURNING MERELY A A FEW FEET AWAY?
BIRBAL, I SEE YOUR POINT. WE WILL GIVE THE REWARD TO THE POOR MAN AS SOON AS WE RETURN TO THE COURT. BUT WE ARE HUNGRY NOW.
JAHANPANAH, I AM SORRY FOR HAVING KEPT YOU HUNGRY FOR SUCH A LONG TIME. THE MEAL WILL BE SERVED IN A SHORT WHILE.
THAT EVENING, THE EMPEROR SUMMONED THE POOR BRAHMAN TO THE COURT AND GAVE HIM THE REWARD.
JAHANPANAH! YOU ARE KIND AND JUST.

THE WICKED KAZI
IN THE DAYS OF AKBAR, THE PEOPLE HAD RESPECT FOR KAZIS, FOR THEY WERE THE OFFICIALS APPOINTED BY THE EMPEROR TO SETTLE DISPUTES. BUT THE KAZI OF DELHI WAS A DISHONEST MAN.
ONE DAY, A POOR WOMAN CAME TO HIM.
SIR, PLEASE KEEP THIS BAG IN YOUR CUSTODY TILL I RETURN FROM MY PILGRIMAGE. IT CONTAINS A THOUSAND GOLD COINS.
HAVE YOU SEALED THE BAG?
YES, I HAVE.

WHEN WILL YOU BE BACK?
I AM LEAVING FOR MECCA. IT IS A LONG WAY OFF. IT MAY TAKE ME A YEAR OR TWO TO RETURN.
I DO NOT LIKE TO HAVE ANYTHING TO DO WITH MONEY. BUT I DO NOT WANT TO DISAPPOINT YOU EITHER. SO LEAVE THE BAG AND GO IN PEACE.
THREE YEARS LATER, THE OLD WOMAN RETURNED.
SIR, I THANK YOU FOR KEEPING MY BAG IN YOUR CUSTODY. NOW THAT I AM BACK, PLEASE RETURN IT TO ME.

THE KAZI WENT IN AND BROUGHT THE BAG.
HERE IS YOUR BAG.
INSPECT THE SEAL BEFORE YOU TAKE THE BAG AWAY.
IT'S INTACT. THANK YOU, SIR.
AND THE OLD WOMAN WENT HOME.
THERE, WHEN SHE OPENED THE BAG—
GOOD LORD! THESE ARE ONLY FLAT ROUND STONES! WHAT HAPPENED TO MY GOLD COINS?
SHE CAME WAILING TO THE KAZI.
BIBI, I DON'T KNOW WHAT YOUR BAG CONTAINED. ALL I KNOW IS THAT YOU GAVE ME A SEALED BAG, AND YOU TOOK IT BACK.

THE OLD WOMAN APPEALED TO THE EMPEROR FOR JUSTICE.
JAHANPANAH ! THE BAG CONTAINED ALL MY SAVINGS. I HAVE BEEN CHEATED BY THE KAZI.
THE KAZI STUCK TO HIS STATEMENT.
JAHANPANAH ! THE WOMAN GAVE ME A SEALED BAG. WHEN SHE TOOK IT BACK, THE SEAL WAS INTACT. I HAD NO IDEA WHAT THE BAG CONTAINED.
LATER, WHEN THE EMPEROR WAS ALONE WITH BIRBAL—
JAHANPANAH, IT SEEMS TO ME THAT THE KAZI TORE OPEN THE BAG AND THEN HAD IT DARNED BY A CLEVER DARNER.

NEXT MORNING AS SUGGESTED BY BIRBAL, AKBAR TORE A CORNER OF HIS BEDSHEET.

AT NIGHT, WHEN HE ENTERED THE BED-ROOM —
WHY, THE SHEET HAS BEEN DARNED SO PERFECTLY THAT I JUST CAN'T BELIEVE IT WAS EVER TORN. WHO DARNED IT?

THE SERVANT EXPLAINED.
JAHANPANAH, FOR FEAR OF BEING PUNISHED, I WENT TO THE CLEVEREST DARNER IN THE TOWN.
BRING HIM TO THE COURT TOMORROW.

WHEN THE DARNER APPEARED IN THE COURT NEXT DAY –
TELL ME. WHO ELSE HAS ENGAGED YOUR SERVICES RECENTLY?
THE KAZI SAHAB, JAHANPANAH! I DARNED A BAG CONTAINING STONES FOR HIM.
WHEN THE KAZI WAS SUMMONED TO THE COURT HE WAS FRIGHTENED TO SEE THE DARNER THERE.
JAHANPANAH, I CONFESS. I TOOK THE GOLD BELONGING TO THIS WOMAN.
YOU ARE HEREWITH DISMISSED FROM THE JOB.
AS FOR YOUR PROPERTY, WHATEVER IS LEFT AFTER PAYING THE OLD WOMAN, WILL BE DEPOSITED IN THE ROYAL TREASURY.
JAHANPANAH! YOU ARE JUST AND KIND.

THE MANGO TREE
ONCE TWO FARMERS, RAMU AND SHAMU CAME TO BIRBAL SEEKING JUSTICE.
HUZUR, THERE IS A MANGO TREE ON THE EDGE OF MY FARM. IT HAS ALWAYS BELONGED TO ME. NOW SHAMU CLAIMS IT IS HIS.
HUZUR, THE TREE RIGHTFULLY BELONGS TO ME. I HAVE WATERED IT FROM THE TIME IT WAS A SAPLING.
YOU MAY GO HOME NOW. BUT PRESENT YOURSELVES HERE TOMORROW.
AS SOON AS THE TWO FARMERS LEFT, BIRBAL SENT FOR A TRUSTED SERVANT.
GO TO THEIR HOUSES AT DUSK AND TELL THEM THAT SOME MANGOES ARE BEING STOLEN BY THIEVES. REPORT THEIR REACTIONS TO ME.

WHEN RAMU HEARD THE NEWS—
I HAVE SOME URGENT WORK NOW. I WILL LOOK INTO THE MATTER LATER.
AS SOON AS SHAMU HEARD THE NEWS HE RAN OUT TOWARDS THE TREE WITH A STICK IN HIS HAND.
THE NEXT DAY AT BIRBAL'S COURT—
THE TREE OBVIOUSLY CANNOT BELONG TO BOTH OF YOU. PLEASE TELL ME THE TRUTH — TO WHOM DOES IT BELONG?
TO ME!
TO ME!
SINCE I FIND IT DIFFICULT TO SETTLE THIS DISPUTE, I ORDER THAT THE MANGOES BE PLUCKED AND DIVIDED EQUALLY BETWEEN THE TWO OF YOU.

AS FOR THE TREE, IT WILL BE CUT DOWN AND THE WOOD, TOO, WILL BE EQUALLY DIVIDED.
RAMU FELT HAPPY AT THIS JUDGEMENT.
YOU ARE FAIR AND JUST.
HUZUR, I HAVE TENDED THAT TREE FOR SEVEN YEARS. I CAN'T SEE IT HEWN DOWN. LET THE TREE GO TO RAMU.
SHAMU, I DECLARE YOU TO BE THE RIGHTFUL OWNER. LET RAMU BE WHIPPED FOR TELLING A LIE.

AMAR CHITRA KATHA

Birbal the Witty

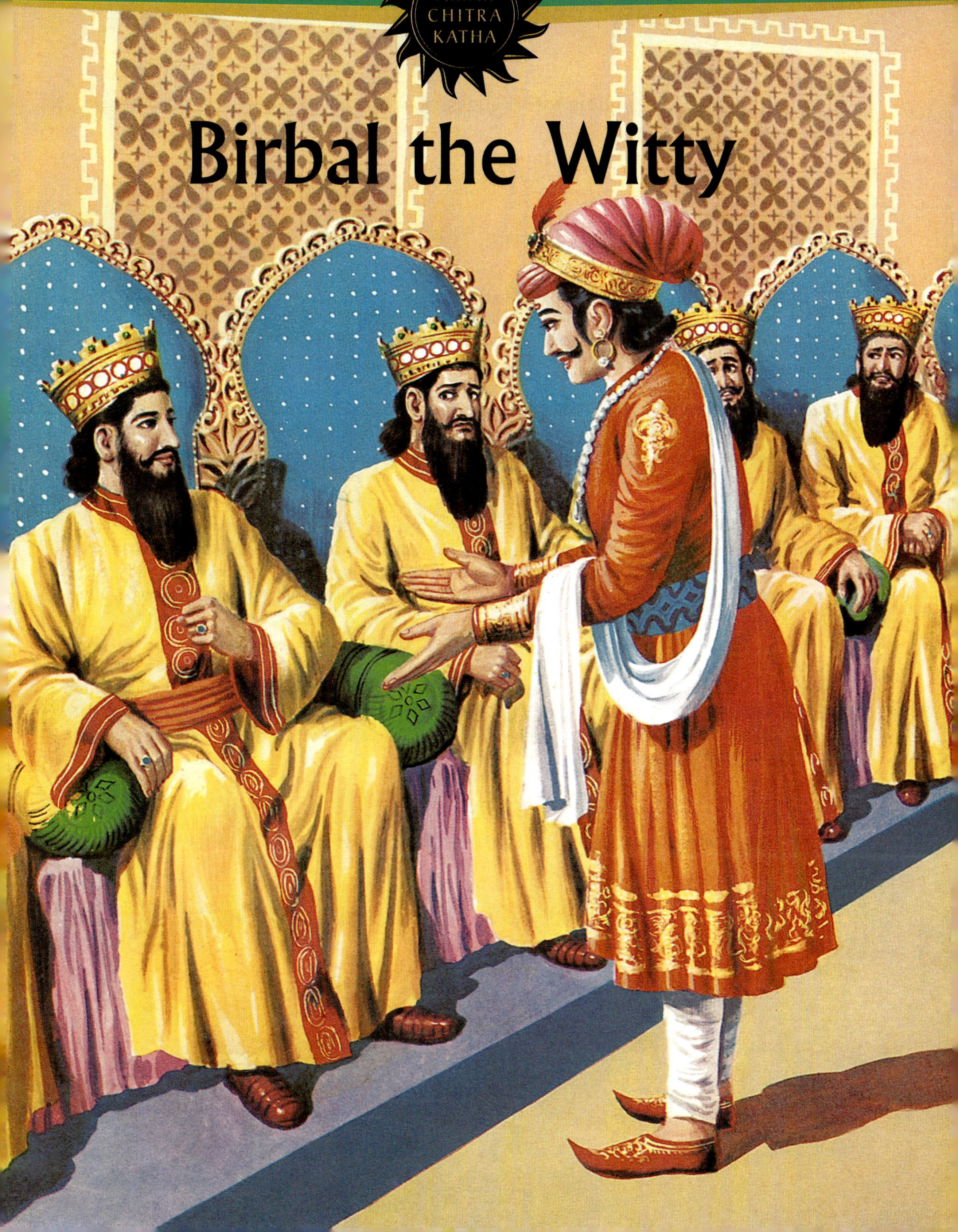

Illustrated Classics From India

Birbal The Witty

Birbal's sharp intellect saw him rise to a prominent position as a minister in the court of the Mughal Emperor Akbar. His wit and wisdom endeared him not only to Akbar, but also to a vast majority of the subjects of the Mughal Empire. He had the rare distinction of achieving immense popularity during his lifetime, next only to that of Akbar. He was a fair administrator, a brave soldier and, perhaps what pleased Akbar the most, a good jester.

This Amar Chitra Katha narrates some amusing anecdotes of Birbal's quick humour, sharp thinking, and his witty repartees with Akbar, who would often challenge Birbal with the strangest of things. In these stories, Birbal hunts down the ten greatest fools in the kingdom, counts the crows of Agra, impresses even the Shah of Persia and manages to point out Akbar's flaws to him with tact and subtlety.

The fact that Birbal was also a good poet is little known. He wrote under the pen name 'Brahma' and a collection of his poems is preserved in the Bharatpur Museum. Though popularly known as Birbal, his real name was Maheshdas. It is believed that he belonged to a poor Brahmin family of Trivikrampur (now known as Tikawanpur), on the banks of the River Yamuna. His phenomenal success made many courtiers jealous and, if popular accounts are to be believed, they were constantly plotting against him.

According to legend, even his death, while leading a large military expedition to Afghanistan, was a result of treachery. Though he was killed in battle, the expedition was successful and managed to subdue the turbulent province. Akbar was so moved when he heard of Birbal's death that he burst forth into a couplet and lamented, "Birbal, you never hurt the helpless. You always gave them whatever you had. I am helpless now and yet you have left nothing for me." Akbar found in Birbal a true friend and sympathiser.

Script: Kamala Chandrakant   Illustrations: Ram Waeerkar   Cover: C M Vitankar

THE TEN GREATEST FOOLS
AS THE EMPEROR, I MEET ONLY WISE AND LEARNED MEN, BIRBAL, NEVER A FOOL. SHOW ME THE TEN GREATEST FOOLS IN THE CITY.
AKBAR OFTEN ASKED BIRBAL TO DO THE STRANGEST OF THINGS, BUT THIS ONE BEAT THEM ALL.
I'LL GIVE YOU A MONTH TO FIND THEM.
IT SHOULD BE NO PROBLEM, JAHANPANAH. I MAY NOT NEED ALL THAT TIME.
AS BIRBAL WENT ABOUT THE CITY LOOKING FOR FOOLS, HE CAME UPON A STRANGE SIGHT.
WHY DO YOU CARRY THAT BUNDLE ON YOUR HEAD INSTEAD OF PLACING IT BEHIND YOU, ON THE SADDLE?

MY HORSE IS OLD AND FEEBLE, HUZUR.* THIS WOOD MIGHT PROVE TOO HEAVY FOR HIM. HE MIGHT FALL DEAD! SO I'M CARRYING IT FOR HIM.
THERE CAN BE NO GREATER FOOL THAN THIS ONE!
COME WITH ME, MY MAN, AND YOU'LL NEVER HAVE TO CARRY ANOTHER BUNDLE IN YOUR LIFE.
AS THE TWO RODE ON, THEY SAW A MAN LYING FLAT ON HIS BACK WITH HIS ARMS IN THE AIR.
?
!

* SIR

WHY, THAT MAN SEEMS TO HAVE HAD A STROKE! WAIT HERE WHILE I HELP HIM SIT UP.
NO! DON'T! PLEASE DON'T TOUCH MY HANDS!
I'M SORRY! DO THEY HURT?
NO! NO! NOT AT ALL! MY WIFE HAS ASKED ME TO BUY A POT AS BIG AS THIS.

IF I MOVE MY HANDS, I'LL GET THE WRONG SIZE; AND MY WIFE, A TERRIBLE SHREW, WILL SCOLD ME FOR THE REST OF MY LIFE.
WHAT A PRIZE FOOL! I MUST TAKE HIM WITH ME.
BIRBAL HELPED HIM UP, WITHOUT TOUCHING HIS ARMS.
NOW DROP YOUR ARMS. IF YOU COME WITH ME, I'LL BUY YOU A BEAUTIFUL SET OF POTS; FROM THE SMALLEST TO THE LARGEST SIZE!

AND YOUR WIFE WILL BE SO PLEASED THAT SHE'LL NEVER AGAIN SCOLD YOU !
AS BIRBAL TURNED TO MOUNT HIS HORSE—
WHAT'S THE MATTER WITH YOU ? CAN'T YOU SEE...
A THOUSAND PARDONS, HUZUR. I HAD JUST CALLED THE EVENING PRAYER FROM THAT MOSQUE...

*MUSLIM PRIEST +COINS

CERTAINLY, HUZUR, I'LL COME. HOW CAN A SLAVE DISOBEY HIS MASTER?
TWO GOLD MOHURS!

BIRBAL TOOK THE THREE MEN TO HIS PALACE.
NOW WAIT HERE TILL I RETURN.

BIRBAL DID NOT HAVE TO GO FAR TO FIND MORE FOOLS.
WHAT ARE THOSE MEN UP TO?

WHY ARE YOU QUARRELLING, MY GOOD MEN?
HUZUR, HE THREATENS TO SET HIS TIGER ON MY BUFFALO!
BUT I SEE NEITHER TIGER NOR BUFFALO!
YOU WILL, IF GOD APPEARS BEFORE US AND CHOOSES TO GIVE US A BOON EACH.
DID YOU HEAR THAT? NOW DO YOU BELIEVE ME? HE KEEPS SAYING THAT IF I ASK GOD FOR A BUFFALO, HE WILL ASK FOR A TIGER TO EAT UP MY BUFFALO.

AND I WILL, TOO!
OH! WILL YOU? TAKE THAT AND THAT!
FOOLS! STOP IT! I SAY STOP IT!
HUZUR!
THE NEXT MOMENT, BIRBAL RECOVERED HIS COMPOSURE.
WHAT'S HAPPENING TO ME?
WHAT A FOOL YOU ARE, HUZUR, TO TAKE THESE FOOLS SERIOUSLY!
IF YOU AREN'T, LET MY BONES BREAK TO BITS AND MY BLOOD RUN...
...LIKE THIS OIL!

ALAS! WHAT HAVE I DONE! WHAT A WASTE OF A GOOD JAR AND PURE OIL!

WITHOUT A WORD, BIRBAL MARCHED THE THREE MEN OFF TO HIS PALACE ...

...AND LEFT THEM WITH THE OTHER THREE FOOLS.

IT WAS ALMOST DARK. THE DAY'S EXPERIENCES HAD PROVED TOO MUCH, EVEN FOR BIRBAL.
I'D BETTER GO OUT AND GET SOME FRESH AIR. I'LL LOOK FOR MORE FOOLS TOMORROW.

A FEW HOURS LATER, AS A REFRESHED BIRBAL WAS ON HIS WAY BACK TO HIS PALACE—
WHAT A BEAUTIFUL MOON! EVEN A THOUSAND LAMPS WOULD NOT LIGHT UP THE STREET AS IT DOES!

WHAT ARE YOU LOOKING FOR?
MY RING, HUZUR.

DID YOU DROP IT HERE?
NO HUZUR, OVER THERE, UNDER THAT TREE. BUT IT'S BRIGHTER HERE, SO I'M LOOKING FOR IT HERE.
COME WITH ME, AND I'LL BUY YOU A NEW RING.
OH! HOW KIND YOU ARE, HUZUR!
AS BIRBAL, LOST IN THE BEAUTY OF THE MOONLIT NIGHT, WALKED ON—
HUZUR! HUZUR! LOOK! THERE IS ANOTHER MAN WHO ALSO SEEMS TO BE SEARCHING FOR SOMETHING.
WH...WHAT?

LET US HELP HIM, HUZUR.
OH! YES, CERTAINLY. WHY NOT!
THEY WALKED UP TO THE MAN.
AH! HUZUR! PERHAPS YOU CAN HELP ME.
I HID MY RING FOR SAFE-KEEPING, IN A HOLE IN THIS SAND-PILE, AND NOW I CAN'T FIND IT.
YOU MUST HAVE MARKED THE SPOT, I SUPPOSE.

BUT NATURALLY, HUZUR! I AM NOT SUCH A FOOL. THERE WAS A CLOUD RIGHT ABOVE THE SPOT WHERE I HID THE RING.
NOW THE TREACHEROUS CLOUD HAS GONE AND SO HAS MY RING!
HE'S RIGHT, HUZUR! HOW WAS HE TO KNOW THAT THE CLOUD WOULD BETRAY HIM SO CRUELLY?
NEVER MIND THE CLOUD. COME WITH ME. WE WILL REPLACE YOUR RING.
YOU DON'T MEAN IT, HUZUR!
HE DOES! HE IS THE KINDEST MAN I'VE EVER MET.

BACK AT HIS PALACE—
THERE! I HAVE EIGHT OF THEM! FOR THE NINTH AND THE TENTH... WELL!
THE NEXT MORNING, BIRBAL ENTERED THE COURT WITH THE FOOLS.
WHAT! BACK SO SOON, BIRBAL?
IT'S NOT SURPRISING, JAHANPANAH. EVERY-ONE KNOWS THAT FOOLS ARE EASIER FOUND THAN WISE MEN.
AND BIRBAL TOLD THE EMPEROR ABOUT HIS ENCOUNTER WITH EACH OF THEM.
BUT THERE ARE ONLY EIGHT FOOLS HERE! I DISTINCTLY REMEMBER ASKING YOU TO SHOW ME TEN.
I BEG TO CORRECT YOU, JAHANPANAH. THERE **ARE** TEN.

THESE EIGHT AND, PARDON ME FOR SAYING SO, JAHANPANAH, THE TWO OF US!
WHAT?
YES, JEHANPANAH. WE HAVE BEEN THE BIGGEST FOOLS OF THEM ALL! YOU FOR SENDING ME ON SUCH AN ERRAND AND I FOR OBEYING YOU.
THE WHOLE COURT BURST OUT LAUGHING; BUT THE LOUDEST LAUGH WAS THAT OF THE EMPEROR, WHO WAS RENOWNED FOR HIS FINE SENSE OF HUMOUR.
HA HA
HA HA HA
HA
HA HA
HO HO
HO
HA HA HA

THE CROWS OF AGRA
ONE DAY, AKBAR'S COURTIERS CAME TO HIM WITH A COMPLAINT.
JAHANPANAH, WHY DO YOU ALWAYS TURN TO BIRBAL WHEN YOU HAVE A PROBLEM?
BECAUSE HE HAS AN ANSWER FOR EVERYTHING– A SOLUTION FOR EVERY PROBLEM.
SO DO WE. BUT YOU NEVER GIVE US A CHANCE.
AH! HERE COMES BIRBAL. ALL RIGHT, TODAY I WILL GIVE ALL OF YOU A CHANCE.

AS SOON AS BIRBAL JOINED THEM, AKBAR LOOKED UP INTO THE SKY.
I WOULD LIKE TO KNOW HOW MANY CROWS WE HAVE IN AGRA.
THE COURTIERS LOOKED AT ONE ANOTHER IN DISMAY.
HOW ARE WE TO KNOW ?
IT WOULD TAKE US YEARS TO FIND OUT.
IT WOULD BE IMPOSSIBLE TO COUNT THEM, JAHANPANAH! THEY DON'T STAY IN ONE PLACE.
NOBODY CAN ANSWER THAT QUESTION, JAHANPANAH. NOT EVEN BIRBAL!
AKBAR LOOKED AT BIRBAL.
THERE ARE THIRTY-THREE THOUSAND, NINE HUNDRED AND TWENTY-ONE, TO BE EXACT.
HIS PROMPT, CONFIDENT ANSWER AMAZED EVEN THE EMPEROR.
BIRBAL! HOW CAN YOU BE SO SURE? YOU WILL BE SEVERELY PUNISHED IF YOU ARE WRONG.
I AM CONFIDENT THAT I AM RIGHT, JAHANPANAH.

WHAT IF THERE ARE MORE CROWS THAN YOU CLAIM?
THOSE WOULD BE THE CROWS WHO HAVE COME FROM OTHER PARTS TO VISIT THEIR FRIENDS AND RELATIVES IN AGRA. NATURALLY, I CAN'T INCLUDE THEM. FOR THEY WILL SOON GO AWAY.
AND SUPPOSE THERE ARE FEWER THAN YOU CLAIM?
OH, THAT! IT'S SIMPLE. MANY OF OUR CROWS HAVE GONE TO VISIT THEIR FRIENDS AND RELATIVES IN OTHER PARTS. NATURALLY, I HAVE NOT INCLUDED THEM IN MY COUNTING!
AS THE COURTIERS SULKED IN SULLEN SILENCE, AKBAR ADDRESSED THEM TRIUMPHANTLY.
THAT'S WHY I SAY, BIRBAL HAS AN ANSWER FOR EVERYTHING! NOW DO YOU AGREE?

BIRBAL AND THE SHAH OF PERSIA
BIRBAL'S FAME AS THE WISEST, THE WITTIEST OF COURTIERS, HAD REACHED EVEN THE EARS OF THE SHAH OF DISTANT PERSIA.
I MUST INVITE HIM TO MY COURT AND SEE IF HE REALLY IS AS CLEVER AS HIS REPUTATION CLAIMS.

A FEW MONTHS LATER, BIRBAL CAME TO THE PERSIAN CAPITAL.
COME, HUZUR. YOU MAY PAY YOUR RESPECTS TO OUR SHAH. HE IS IMPATIENT TO SEE YOU. LET ME LEAD YOU TO HIS PRESENCE.

AS BIRBAL ENTERED THE SHAH'S DARBAR, A STRANGE SIGHT MET HIS EYES.

WHAT SHOULD HE DO? HE HAD NEVER SEEN THE SHAH BEFORE. AND ALL THESE MEN WERE DRESSED ALIKE AND SAT ON IDENTICAL THRONES!
WHICH ONE OF THEM IS THE SHAH?

FOR A MOMENT, BIRBAL STOOD STILL AND LET HIS GAZE TRAVEL DOWN THE ROW OF THRONES.

WITHOUT A DOUBT, YOU ARE THE SHAH!

OUR EMPEROR SENDS YOUR HIGHNESS HIS REGARDS. HE HAS SENT ME WITH GIFTS WHICH ARE ON THEIR WAY TO THE TREASURY.
THE SHAH WAS AMAZED.
BIRBAL! HOW DID YOU RECOGNIZE ME! YOU'VE NEVER SEEN ME BEFORE!
IT WAS SIMPLE, YOUR HIGHNESS. AS I STOOD PERPLEXED, ALL THE OTHERS TURNED TO LOOK AT YOU TO SEE YOUR REACTION; WHILE YOU LOOKED STRAIGHT AHEAD.
THE SHAH MARVELLED AT BIRBAL'S KEEN SENSE OF OBSERVATION.
YOU ARE INDEED THE CLEVEREST PERSON I HAVE EVER MET!
YOU SHALL HENCEFORTH BE CALLED THE OCEAN OF INTELLIGENCE.
AND BEFORE BIRBAL LEFT FOR HINDUSTAN, THE SHAH GAVE HIM ALL THE RICHES HE COULD CARRY WITH HIM.

THE SEAL
AKBAR HAD THE HABIT OF DISGUISING HIMSELF AND WANDERING ABOUT IN THE CITY — A HABIT BIRBAL DIDN'T APPROVE OF, AS HE THOUGHT IT UNSAFE.
ALL RIGHT, BIRBAL, I'M OFF.
I STILL SAY YOU OUGHT TO GIVE UP THIS HABIT, JAHANPANAH. AN EMPEROR'S LIFE IS PRECIOUS AND MUST BE WELL PROTECTED.
LATER, AS AKBAR WALKED DOWN THE STREET—
I THINK I'M BEING FOLLOWED.

HE STOPPED IN HIS TRACKS AND TURNED ROUND.
THERE! HE'S STOPPED, TOO, AND IS PRETENDING TO LOOK INTO THAT SHOP. I'LL GO UP TO HIM AND QUESTION HIM.
WHAT'S YOUR NAME?
WANDERLUST.
WHAT DO YOU DO FOR A LIVING?
I WANDER!
WHERE DO YOU LIVE?
EVERYWHERE.

SO IRRITATED WAS AKBAR BY THESE ANSWERS THAT HE FORGOT HIMSELF.
DO YOU KNOW WHO I AM?
A HUMAN BEING LIKE ANY OTHER!
I AM THE EMPEROR. HERE IS MY SEAL, IF YOU DON'T BELIEVE ME.
LET ME SEE IT.
THE STRANGER SLIPPED THE RING INTO HIS CUMMERBAND.

ONLY WHEN THE STRANGER BEGAN TO RUN AWAY DID AKBAR REALISE WHAT HE HAD DONE.
THIEF! THIEF! CATCH HIM! CATCH HIM!
A CROWD RAN AFTER THE THIEF.
DON'T LET HIM ESCAPE.
WHEN THEY CAUGHT UP WITH THE MAN–
FOOLS, DON'T YOU KNOW ME? I'M THE EMPEROR.
THIS SHOULD CONVINCE YOU, IF MY WORDS DON'T!

FORGIVE US, JAHANPANAH!
WE WERE IGNORANT AND ACTED ON THE WORDS OF A MADMAN.
I'D BETTER RETURN TO THE PALACE BEFORE THEY ATTACK ME.
ONLY BIRBAL CAN HELP ME BRING THAT THIEF TO BOOK.
BUT HOW CAN I FACE BIRBAL? HE HAS ALWAYS WARNED ME NOT TO GO OUT ALONE.

FILLED WITH SUCH THOUGHTS, AKBAR WALKED INTO HIS CHAMBER.
WHAT'S THIS?
HE OPENED THE PARCEL.
MY SEAL! THE THIEF HAS RETURNED IT! AH! HERE IS A NOTE. AN APOLOGY, NO DOUBT.
IT WAS NO APOLOGY.
HAVEN'T I WARNED YOU THAT IT'S NOT SAFE FOR YOU TO VENTURE INTO THE CITY WITHOUT YOUR GUARDS? WORSE THINGS THAN LOSING YOUR SEAL COULD HAVE HAPPENED TO YOU.
BIRBAL
SO IT WAS BIRBAL! THE ROGUE! HA! HA! HA! BUT I'VE LEARNED MY LESSON.

AKBAR THE GREAT
ONE DAY, IN OPEN COURT, AKBAR WAS TOLD BY A SYCOPHANT THAT HE WAS GREATER EVEN THAN THE LORD OF THE UNIVERSE.
AKBAR THOUGHT ABOUT IT FOR DAYS.
IN WHAT WAY COULD I BE GREATER THAN GOD?
UNABLE TO ANSWER THE QUESTION FOR HIMSELF, HE SET IT TO HIS COURTIERS.
DO YOU THINK I AM GREATER THAN GOD? IF SO, IN WHAT WAY?
WHAT SHALL I SAY?
WHY DIDN'T HE ASK THE MAN WHO SAID IT?
HOW CAN I ANSWER THAT QUESTION WITHOUT EITHER DISPLEASING THE EMPEROR OR TELLING AN UNTRUTH?

WHEN, LOOKING FROM ONE FACE TO ANOTHER, AKBAR DID NOT RECEIVE AN ANSWER...
...HE TURNED TO BIRBAL.
BIRBAL, DO YOU THINK I AM GREATER THAN GOD? AND I WANT THE TRUTH.
WHY JEHANPANAH, BEYOND A DOUBT YOU ARE!
BIRBAL, ARE YOU TRYING TO FLATTER ME?
NOT AT ALL, JAHANPANAH. THERE IS CERTAINLY ONE THING YOU CAN DO THAT GOD CAN'T.

IF YOU WANT TO BANISH A MAN ALL YOU HAVE TO DO IS SEND HIM OUT OF YOUR KINGDOM.
BUT IF THE LORD OF THE UNIVERSE WANTS TO BANISH A MAN WHERE CAN HE SEND HIM?
HAVE I PROVED MY POINT, JAHANPANAH?
AKBAR SMILED.
YOU CERTAINLY HAVE, BIRBAL. AND THANK YOU FOR OPENING MY EYES SO CLEVERLY AND SO TACTFULLY.

AMAR CHITRA KATHA

Gopal the Jester

Illustrated Classics From India

Gopal the Jester

This Amar Chitra Katha contains seven short stories about Gopal Bhand, the clever barber, who could be described as the "Birbal of Bengal". Gopal's native shrewdness helped him turn every situation to his advantage. No wonder he was favoured by King Krishnachandra of Krishnanagar in Bengal, who owed allegiance to the Nawab of Murshidabad. Whenever the eccentric Nawab gave Krishnachandra an impossible assignment, it was Gopal who came to the king's rescue. Stories about him are extremely popular, particularly in Bengal and Bihar.

The stories in this book are varied. In one, Gopal outwits the Nawab, much to the delight of his king, while in another he pilfers sweets from the local sweet shop. From time to time, Gopal traps a group of dacoits, solves the king's dilemmas and even manages to change the flow of conversation in the entire town! Being the king's favourite, however, did not turn his head. He mingled freely with the common people and often helped them too. That explains the popularity of this folk-hero to this day.

Script: Urmila Sinha   Illustrations: Souren Roy

GOPAL MEASURES THE EARTH
GOPAL, THE CLEVER BARBER, HAD FREE ACCESS TO KRISHNA CHANDRA, THE KING OF KRISHNANAGAR IN BENGAL. BUT ONE DAY—
THE KING DOES NOT WISH TO SEE YOU.
THEN I MUST SEE HIM.
I'M HERE, YOUR MAJESTY. YOUR MAJESTY?
DON'T BOTHER ME NOW, GOPAL. I'M WORRIED.
KINGS DON'T WORRY, YOUR MAJESTY! THEY PAY PEOPLE TO DO IT FOR THEM.

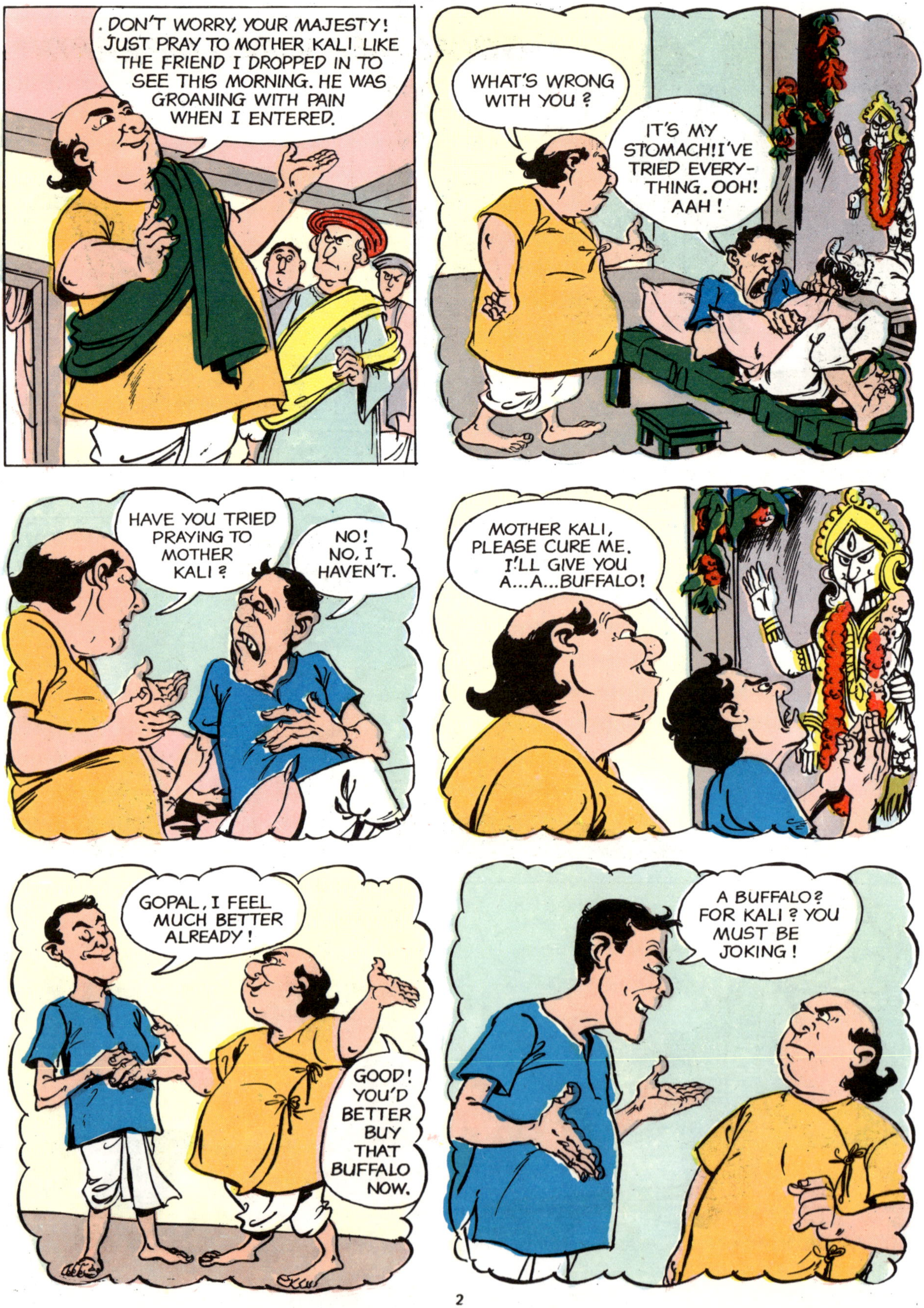
DON'T WORRY, YOUR MAJESTY! JUST PRAY TO MOTHER KALI LIKE THE FRIEND I DROPPED IN TO SEE THIS MORNING. HE WAS GROANING WITH PAIN WHEN I ENTERED.
WHAT'S WRONG WITH YOU ?
IT'S MY STOMACH! I'VE TRIED EVERY-THING. OOH! AAH !
HAVE YOU TRIED PRAYING TO MOTHER KALI ?
NO! NO, I HAVEN'T.
MOTHER KALI, PLEASE CURE ME. I'LL GIVE YOU A...A...BUFFALO!
GOPAL, I FEEL MUCH BETTER ALREADY !
GOOD! YOU'D BETTER BUY THAT BUFFALO NOW.
A BUFFALO? FOR KALI ? YOU MUST BE JOKING !

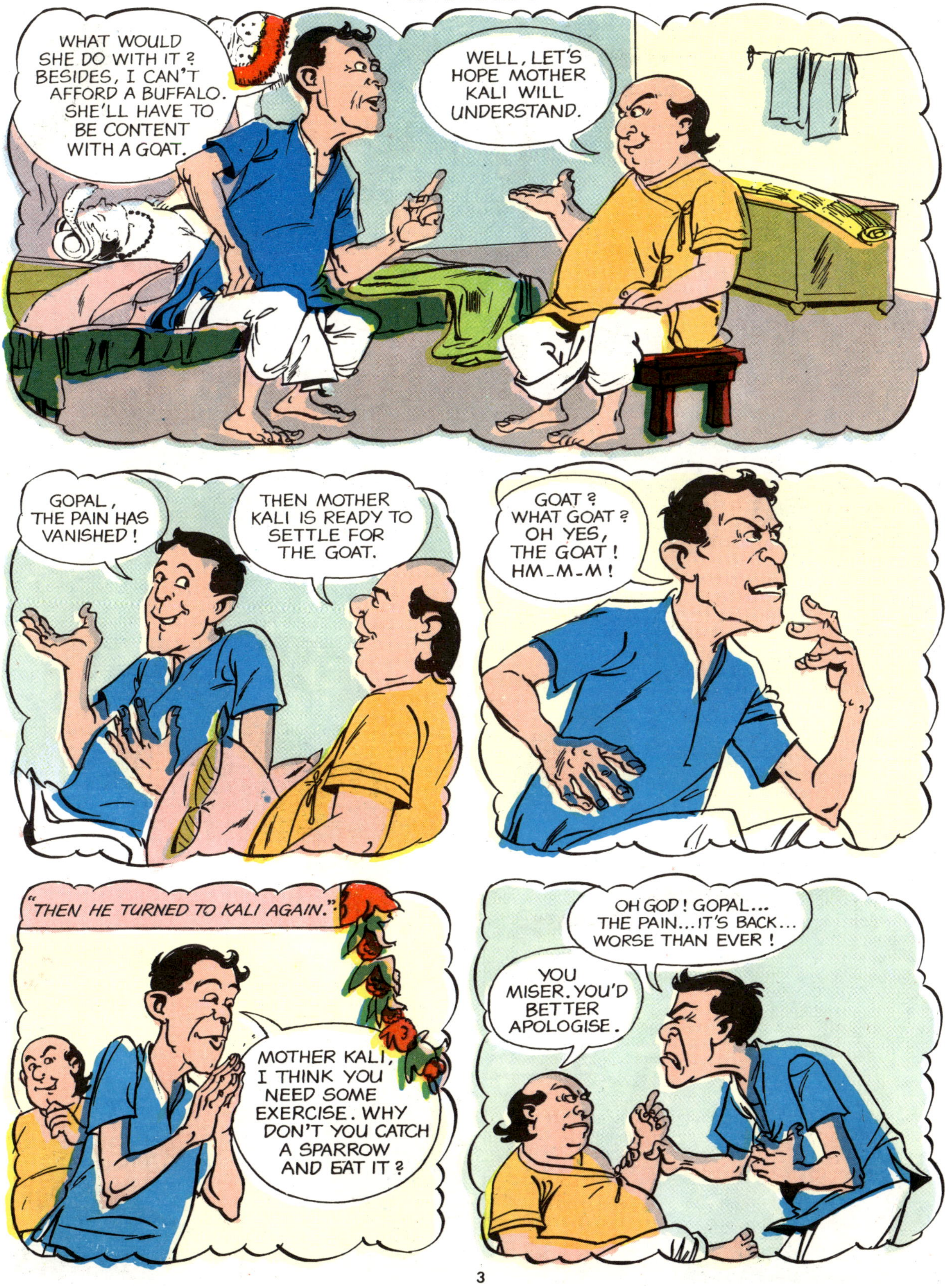
WHAT WOULD SHE DO WITH IT ? BESIDES, I CAN'T AFFORD A BUFFALO. SHE'LL HAVE TO BE CONTENT WITH A GOAT.
WELL, LET'S HOPE MOTHER KALI WILL UNDERSTAND.
GOPAL, THE PAIN HAS VANISHED !
THEN MOTHER KALI IS READY TO SETTLE FOR THE GOAT.
GOAT ? WHAT GOAT ? OH YES, THE GOAT ! HM-M-M !
"THEN HE TURNED TO KALI AGAIN."
MOTHER KALI, I THINK YOU NEED SOME EXERCISE. WHY DON'T YOU CATCH A SPARROW AND EAT IT ?
OH GOD ! GOPAL... THE PAIN... IT'S BACK... WORSE THAN EVER !
YOU MISER. YOU'D BETTER APOLOGISE.

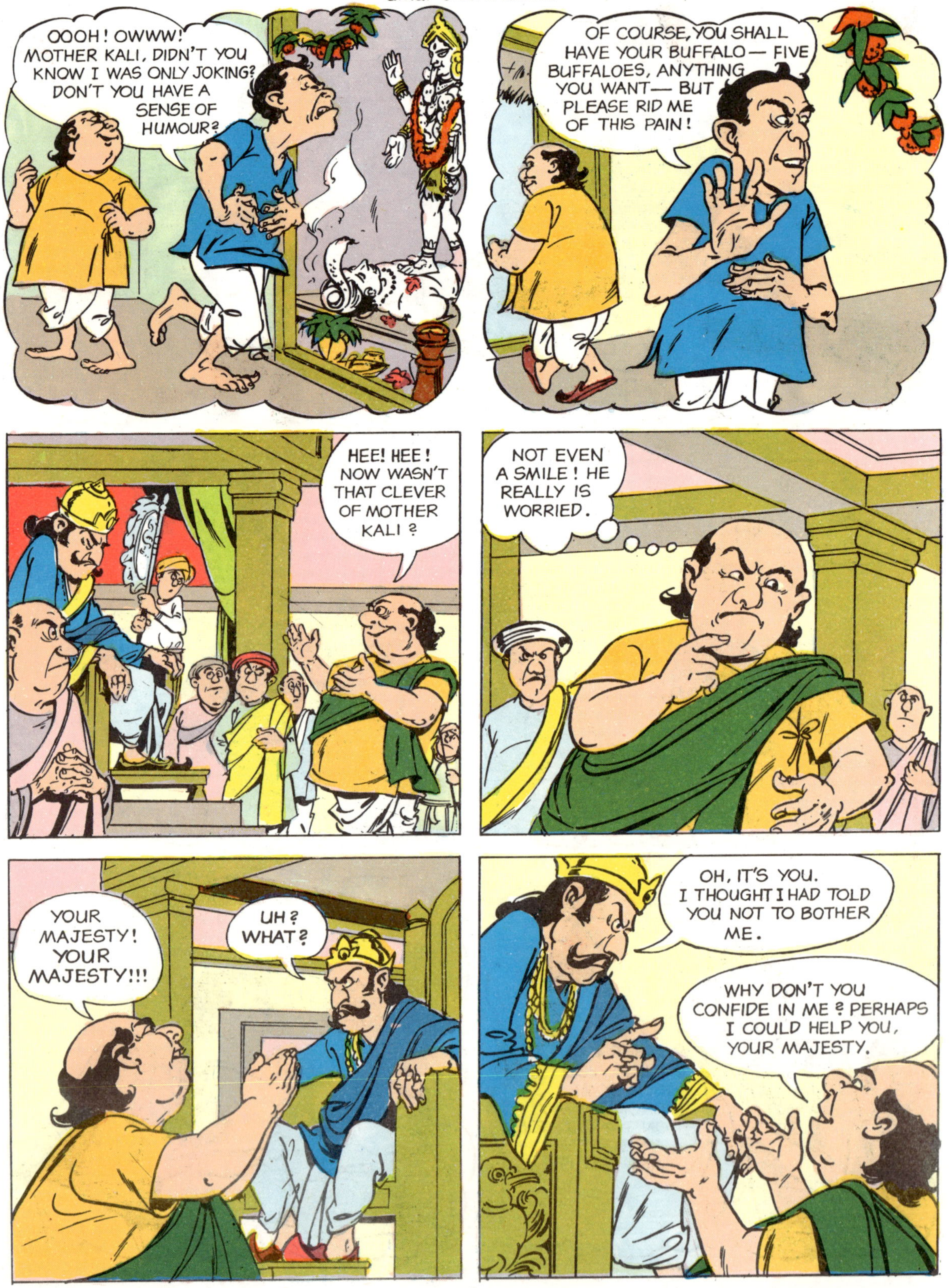
OOOH! OWWW! MOTHER KALI, DIDN'T YOU KNOW I WAS ONLY JOKING? DON'T YOU HAVE A SENSE OF HUMOUR?
OF COURSE, YOU SHALL HAVE YOUR BUFFALO — FIVE BUFFALOES, ANYTHING YOU WANT — BUT PLEASE RID ME OF THIS PAIN!
HEE! HEE! NOW WASN'T THAT CLEVER OF MOTHER KALI?
NOT EVEN A SMILE! HE REALLY IS WORRIED.
YOUR MAJESTY! YOUR MAJESTY!!!
UH? WHAT?
OH, IT'S YOU. I THOUGHT I HAD TOLD YOU NOT TO BOTHER ME.
WHY DON'T YOU CONFIDE IN ME? PERHAPS I COULD HELP YOU, YOUR MAJESTY.

OH, ALL RIGHT! I WILL.
THE NAWAB OF MURSHIDABAD HAS ORDERED ME TO GET SOMEONE TO MEASURE THE LENGTH AND BREADTH OF THE EARTH.
IS THAT ALL ?
ALL ? ALL! WHAT DO YOU MEAN IS THAT ALL ? WHERE AM I TO FIND SOMEONE WHO WILL TAKE ON SUCH AN IMPOSSIBLE TASK ?
RIGHT HERE, YOUR MAJESTY. I'LL DO IT FOR YOU.
DON'T TRY MY PATIENCE, GOPAL !
THIS IS NOT A MATTER TO JOKE ABOUT. PERHAPS MY VERY LIFE IS AT STAKE.
I KNOW, YOUR MAJESTY. THAT'S WHY I SAY, LEAVE IT TO ME.

DO YOU KNOW WHAT WILL HAPPEN IF YOU FAIL? I WILL BE EXECUTED AND YOU WILL BE OUT OF A JOB!
NEITHER OF WHICH WILL HAPPEN, YOUR MAJESTY.
TRUST ME. ALL I'LL NEED IS TWENTY-FIVE BULLOCK CARTS.
BULLOCK CARTS?
YES. AND ALL THE SILK AND COTTON THREAD IN TOWN.
SO, A FEW DAYS LATER GOPAL LEFT FOR MURSHIDABAD AT THE HEAD OF A ROW OF BULLOCK CARTS.
WHEN HE REACHED THE NAWAB'S PALACE AT MURSHIDABAD —
YOU WAIT HERE. I'LL GO AND MEET THE NAWAB.
FROM KRISHNA CHANDRA DID YOU SAY?
YES, YOUR EXCELLENCY.

WHERE ARE THE MEASUREMENTS?
IF YOU STEP OUTSIDE FOR A MOMENT, I'LL GIVE THEM TO YOU, YOUR EXCEL-LENCY.
GOPAL TOOK THE NAWAB TO THE CARTS.
THE THREAD IN THE FIRST FOURTEEN CARTS PUT TOGETHER...
...IS THE LENGTH OF THE EARTH — AND THE REMAINING ELEVEN CART-LOADS, THE BREADTH.
BUT... BUT... WHAT IF IT ISN'T ACCURATE?
YOU COULD HAVE IT CHECKED. OR BETTER STILL, YOUR EXCELLENCY COULD PERSONALLY CHECK IT,

I...I...UH...OH... ALL RIGHT! YOU MAY GO.
BUT, YOUR EXCELLENCY, DON'T I DESERVE A REWARD FOR THE TROUBLE I'VE TAKEN?
WHAT ARE YOU STANDING THERE FOR? GIVE THIS MAN A HUNDRED GOLD COINS!
AT ONCE, YOUR EXCELLENCY.
LATER AT KRISHNA NAGAR—
HA, HA, HA! I MUST SAY YOU'VE DONE VERY WELL, GOPAL. I WISH I'D SEEN HIS FACE.
IT WASN'T EXACTLY A PRETTY SIGHT, YOUR MAJESTY!

GOPAL IN THE SWEET-SHOP
THE CHILDREN OF THE TOWN LOVED GOPAL FOR HE OFTEN JOINED THEM IN THEIR PRANKS. ONE SUMMER AFTERNOON–
WILL YOU DO SOMETHING FOR US?
I'M SURE HE WILL!
WILL YOU GET US SOME FREE SWEETS FROM BHOLA'S SWEET SHOP?
FREE SWEETS FROM THAT MAN? IMPOSSIBLE!
THE MAN CHEATS US EVEN WHEN WE PAY FOR THE SWEETS.
IS THAT SO? WELL, LEAVE HIM TO ME THEN AND GET READY FOR A FEAST!
IT'S ALMOST TIME FOR BHOLA'S AFTERNOON NAP.

TRUE ENOUGH, IT WAS.
I AM GOING IN FOR A NAP. WAKE ME UP IF ANYONE COMES AND DON'T LET ME CATCH YOU EATING THE SWEETS!
YES, FATHER.
WH-WHO ARE YOU? WHAT ARE YOU DOING? STOP IT!
DON'T WORRY. YOUR FATHER KNOWS ME. YOU CAN TELL HIM I'M HERE!
BUT WHO ARE YOU?
JUST CALL ME MAKKHI.*

* A FLY

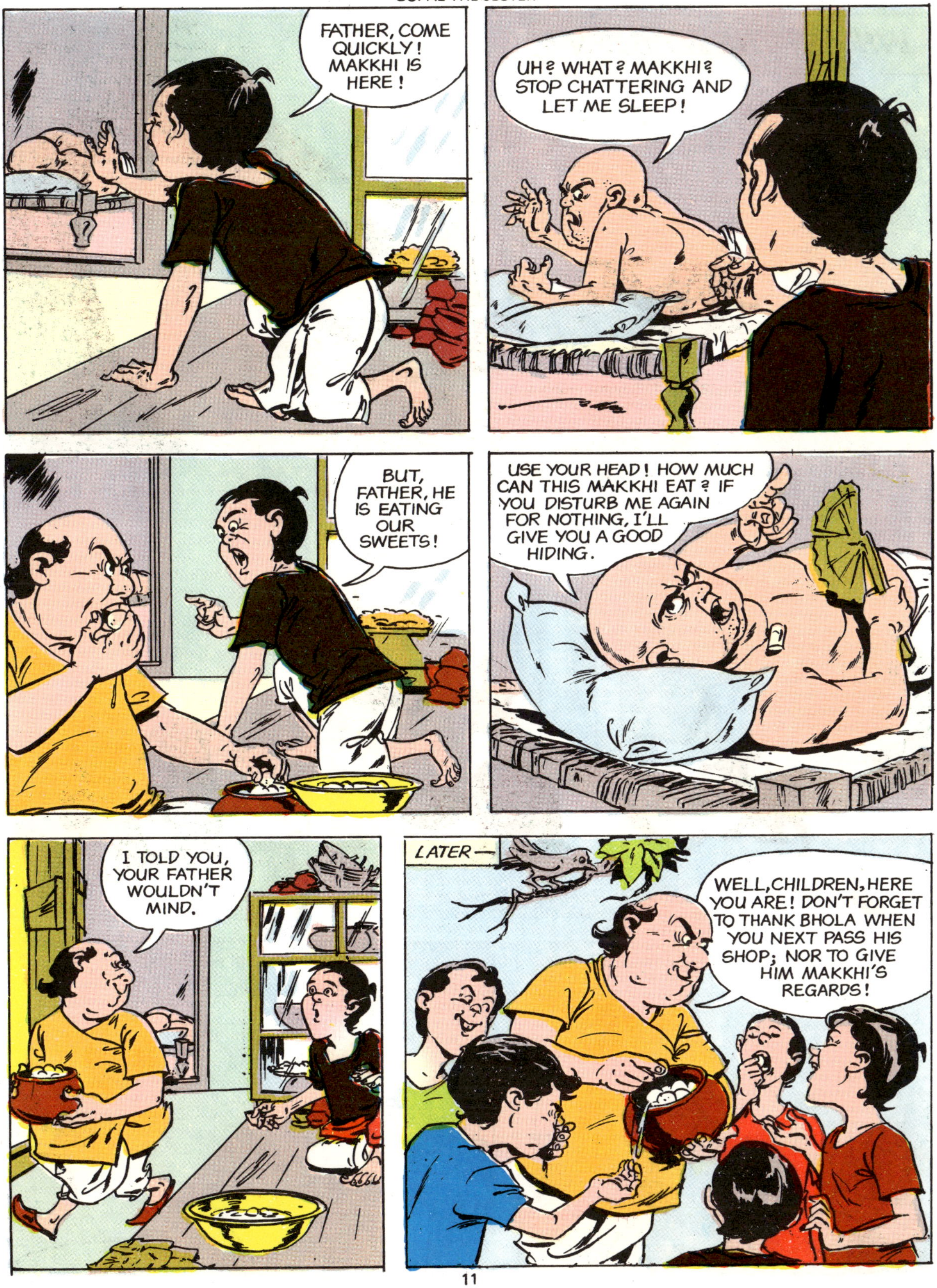
FATHER, COME QUICKLY! MAKKHI IS HERE!
UH? WHAT? MAKKHI? STOP CHATTERING AND LET ME SLEEP!
BUT, FATHER, HE IS EATING OUR SWEETS!
USE YOUR HEAD! HOW MUCH CAN THIS MAKKHI EAT? IF YOU DISTURB ME AGAIN FOR NOTHING, I'LL GIVE YOU A GOOD HIDING.
I TOLD YOU, YOUR FATHER WOULDN'T MIND.
LATER—
WELL, CHILDREN, HERE YOU ARE! DON'T FORGET TO THANK BHOLA WHEN YOU NEXT PASS HIS SHOP; NOR TO GIVE HIM MAKKHI'S REGARDS!

WHO IS THE MASTER ?
ONE DAY, GOPAL WAS ABOUT TO ENTER A SHOP WHEN THE SHOPKEEPER CAME UP BEHIND HIM.
HEY, GOPAL ! KEEP YOUR DOG OUT OF MY SHOP !
MY DOG ?
BUT THIS DOG ISN'T MINE.
NOT YOURS ? OF COURSE IT IS ! YOU ARE ITS MASTER.
IT WAS FOLLOWING YOU, WASN'T IT ?
I SEE. THEN MY DOG MUST BE YOUR MASTER SINCE YOU WERE FOLLOWING IT !
AND IF YOU WANT TO KEEP YOUR MASTER OUT, DO IT YOURSELF.

GOPAL AND THE THIEF
ONE NIGHT A THIEF BROKE INTO GOPAL'S HOUSE.
HAND OVER ALL YOUR GOLD ORNAMENTS! AND BE QUICK!
T...TAKE WHATEVER YOU WANT. B...BUT SPARE OUR LIVES.
JUST THEN THEY HEARD A SOUND.
WHAT'S THAT?
IT MUST BE ANOTHER THIEF TRYING TO BREAK IN.
WHO IS IT?
HUSH! QUIET!
WHAT'S THE MATTER? YOU LOOK WORRIED.
I'M DONE FOR! IT'S A GANG OF DACOITS.

THEY'LL BE HERE ANY MOMENT. THEY'LL MURDER ME. PLEASE PROTECT ME.
WHAT ABOUT US?
CALM DOWN, DEAR. GOD IS PROTECTING US.
ALL RIGHT! DON'T PANIC. WE'LL HIDE YOU TILL THEY'VE GONE.
OH, THANK YOU, SIR, THANK YOU.
NOW STAY THERE AND DON'T EVEN BREATHE. WE'LL GET RID OF THEM.
QUICK, COME WITH ME!
I'M OFF TO GET HELP. NOW LISTEN CAREFULLY AND DO EXACTLY AS I TELL YOU...

GOPAL LEFT BY THE FRONT DOOR.
PLEASE COME BACK SOON.
I WILL. DON'T FORGET TO DO EXACTLY AS I'VE TOLD YOU.
EVEN AS GOPAL'S WIFE CLOSED THE FRONT DOOR, THE DACOITS BROKE IN THROUGH THE BACK DOOR.
COME ON, WOMAN! OUT WITH YOUR GOLD IF YOU VALUE YOUR LIFE!
BUT...BUT...IT'S ALL LOCKED UP.
WHERE ARE THE KEYS?
WITH... WITH THE... MASTER!

WHERE IS HE?
THERE!
OUT WITH THE KEYS, YOU COWARD!
BUT...BUT... BUT I DON'T HAVE THEM!
THE MASTER OF THE HOUSE AND YOU DON'T HAVE THEM! HAND THEM OVER OR ELSE...
PLEASE, DON'T HURT ME...I AM NOT THE MASTER... BELIEVE ME...

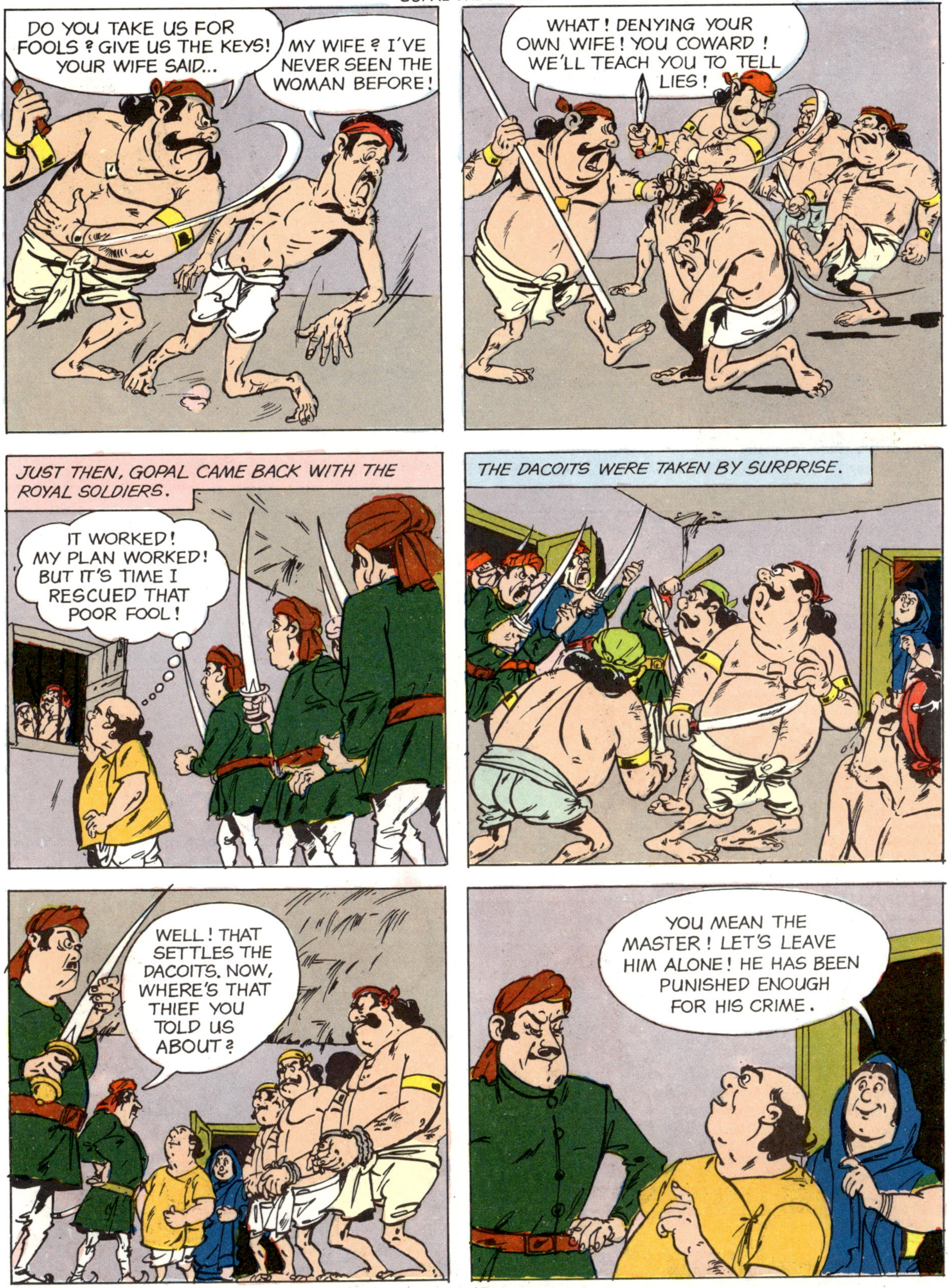
DO YOU TAKE US FOR FOOLS ? GIVE US THE KEYS! YOUR WIFE SAID...
MY WIFE ? I'VE NEVER SEEN THE WOMAN BEFORE!
WHAT ! DENYING YOUR OWN WIFE ! YOU COWARD ! WE'LL TEACH YOU TO TELL LIES !
JUST THEN, GOPAL CAME BACK WITH THE ROYAL SOLDIERS.
IT WORKED! MY PLAN WORKED! BUT IT'S TIME I RESCUED THAT POOR FOOL!
THE DACOITS WERE TAKEN BY SURPRISE.
WELL ! THAT SETTLES THE DACOITS. NOW, WHERE'S THAT THIEF YOU TOLD US ABOUT ?
YOU MEAN THE MASTER ! LET'S LEAVE HIM ALONE ! HE HAS BEEN PUNISHED ENOUGH FOR HIS CRIME.

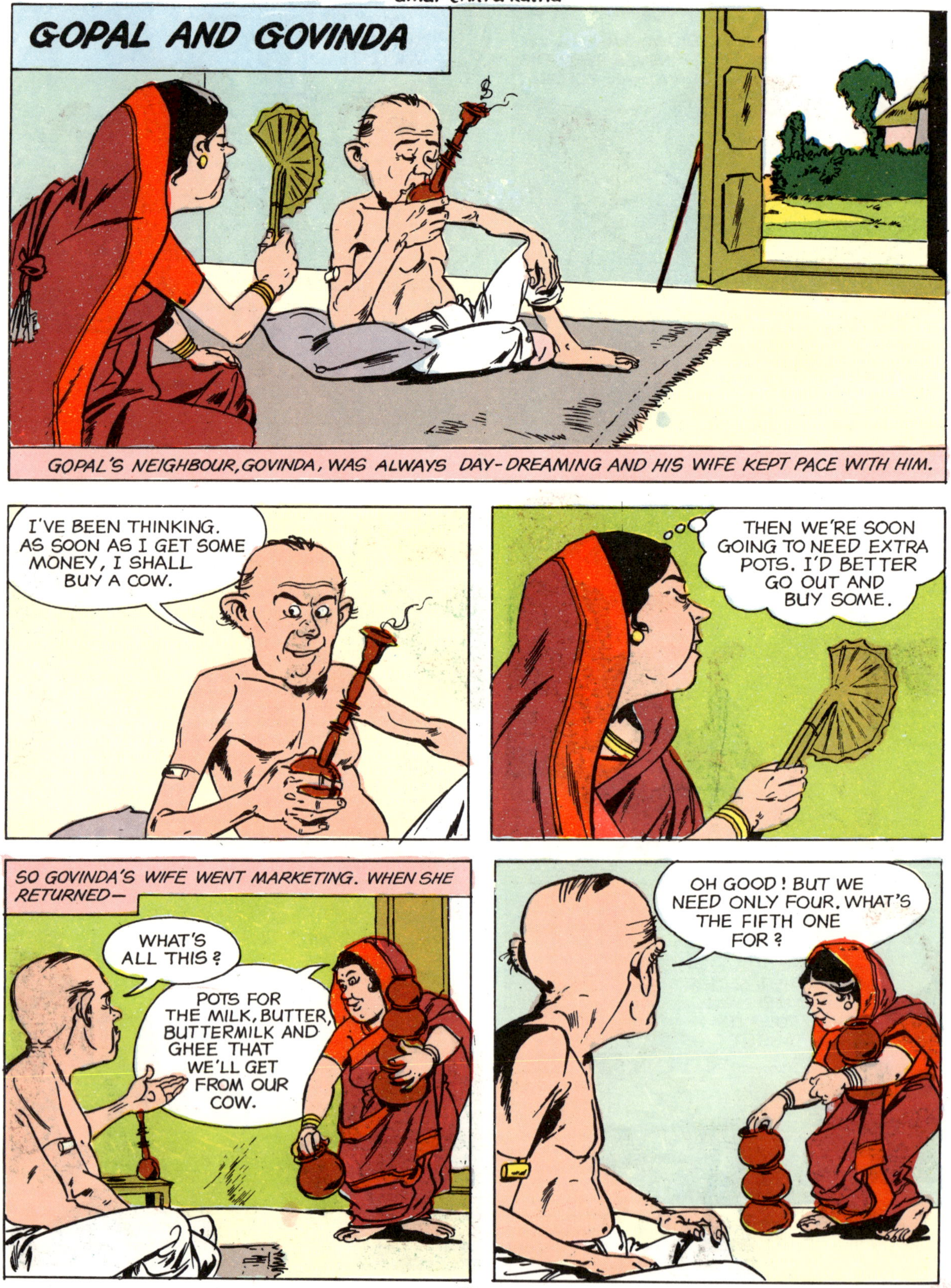
GOPAL AND GOVINDA
GOPAL'S NEIGHBOUR, GOVINDA, WAS ALWAYS DAY-DREAMING AND HIS WIFE KEPT PACE WITH HIM.
I'VE BEEN THINKING. AS SOON AS I GET SOME MONEY, I SHALL BUY A COW.
THEN WE'RE SOON GOING TO NEED EXTRA POTS. I'D BETTER GO OUT AND BUY SOME.
SO GOVINDA'S WIFE WENT MARKETING. WHEN SHE RETURNED—
WHAT'S ALL THIS ?
POTS FOR THE MILK, BUTTER, BUTTERMILK AND GHEE THAT WE'LL GET FROM OUR COW.
OH GOOD ! BUT WE NEED ONLY FOUR. WHAT'S THE FIFTH ONE FOR ?

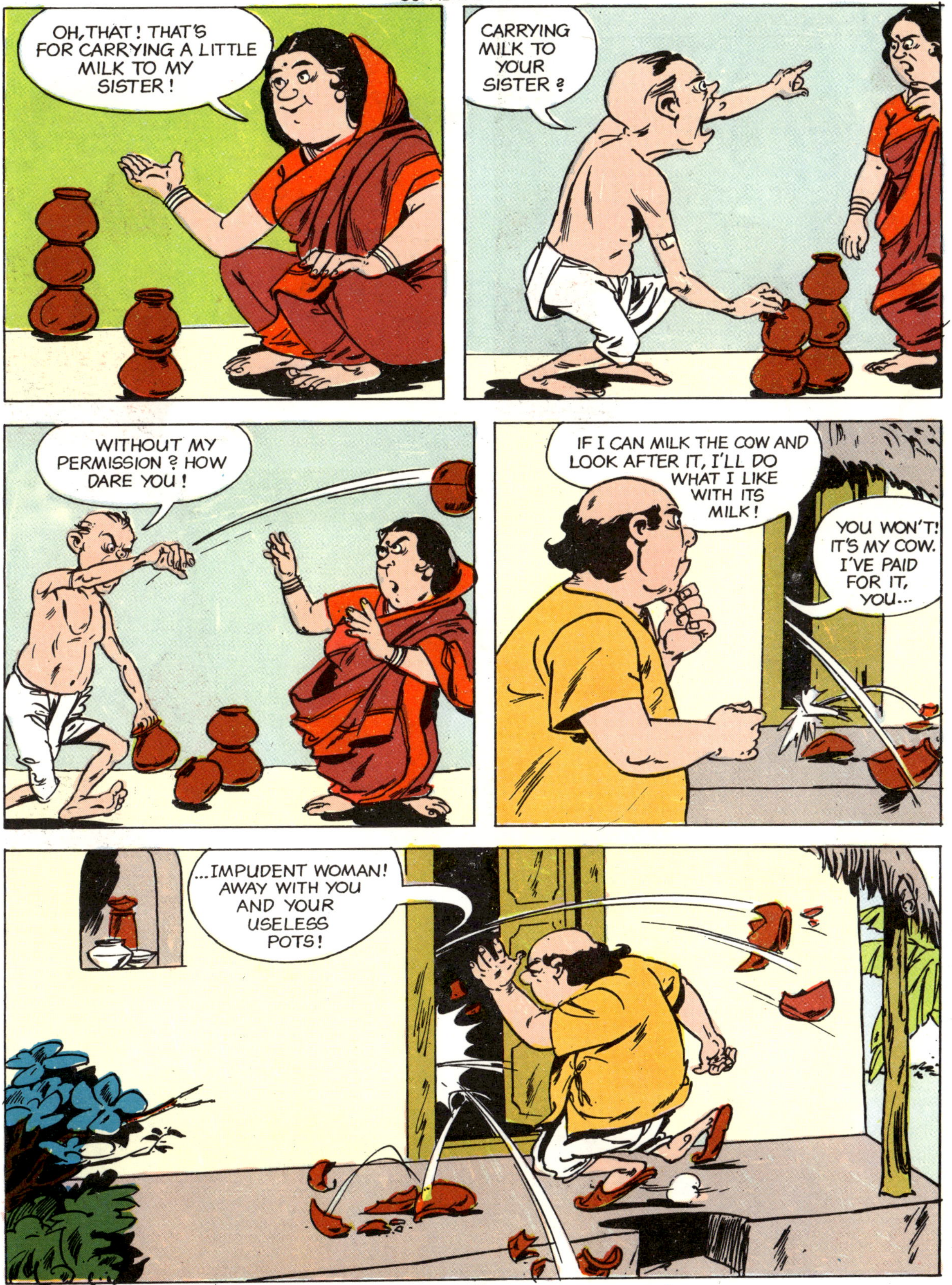
OH, THAT! THAT'S FOR CARRYING A LITTLE MILK TO MY SISTER!
CARRYING MILK TO YOUR SISTER ?
WITHOUT MY PERMISSION ? HOW DARE YOU!
IF I CAN MILK THE COW AND LOOK AFTER IT, I'LL DO WHAT I LIKE WITH ITS MILK!
YOU WON'T! IT'S MY COW. I'VE PAID FOR IT, YOU...
...IMPUDENT WOMAN! AWAY WITH YOU AND YOUR USELESS POTS!

GOPAL RUSHED INTO GOVINDA'S HOUSE.
NOW! NOW! STOP IT!
WHAT ON EARTH IS THE MATTER?
THIS WOMAN IS GOING TO GIVE OUR COW'S MILK AWAY TO HER SISTER!
YOUR COW? WHICH COW?
THE COW I'M GOING TO BUY WHEN I HAVE THE MONEY.
OH! I SEE. BUT YOU DON'T HAVE A COW YET!

SO WHAT? I'M GOING TO GET ONE.
ARE YOU, REALLY ? ALL RIGHT ! WAIT !
HEY! HEY! WHAT ARE YOU DOING ? WHAT HAVE I DONE ?
YOU HAVEN'T DONE ANYTHING. IT'S YOUR COW. IT HAS EATEN THE CABBAGES I AM GOING TO PLANT IN MY GARDEN.
GOING..TO..PLANT...? ALL RIGHT. ALL RIGHT. I REALISE HOW FOOLISH I'VE BEEN ! THANKS TO YOU, GOPAL !

GOPAL AND THE HILSA-FISH
IT WAS THE SEASON FOR HILSA-FISH. FISHERMEN COULD THINK OF NOTHING BUT HILSA-FISH.
FISHMONGERS SOLD NOTHING BUT HILSA-FISH.
COME, BUY. THE PRICE OF HILSA IS DOWN TODAY.
HOUSEHOLDERS COULD TALK OF NOTHING BUT HILSA-FISH.
HOW MUCH DID YOU PAY FOR THAT HILSA ?
YOU WOULDN'T BELIEVE IT IF I TOLD YOU.
AND IN THE PALACE TOO THE COURTIERS COULD DISCUSS NOTHING BUT HILSA-FISH.
YOUR MAJESTY, YOU SHOULD HAVE SEEN THE HUGE HILSA I CAUGHT. IT WAS...

STOP IT!
ARE YOU A COURTIER OR A FISHERMAN?
THE COURTIER FELL SILENT WITH DOWNCAST EYES. THE KING FELT GUILTY.
I'M SORRY I LOST MY TEMPER. IT IS THE SEASON FOR HILSA-FISH AND NO ONE...
...NOT EVEN GOPAL CAN STOP ANYONE FROM TALKING ABOUT HILSA-FISH. NOT EVEN FOR FIVE MINUTES!
OH, I THINK I COULD, YOUR MAJESTY.
THEN LET ME SEE YOU BUY A HUGE HILSA AND BRING IT TO THE PALACE WITHOUT ANYONE ASKING YOU A WORD ABOUT IT!
I ACCEPT THE CHALLENGE, YOUR MAJESTY.

A FEW DAYS LATER—
WHY IS YOUR FACE HALF-SHAVEN?
I'M DRESSING UP TO BUY A FISH.
WHAT'S THE MATTER WITH YOU? WHY ARE YOU SMEARING YOURSELF WITH ASH?
I TOLD YOU— I'M DRESSING UP TO BUY A HILSA-FISH.
LISTEN TO ME! PLEASE. YOU CAN'T POSSIBLY GO OUT IN THOSE DISGRACEFUL RAGS! WHAT ARE YOU UP TO?
HOW MANY TIMES MUST I TELL YOU, WOMAN? I AM OUT TO BUY A HUGE HILSA-FISH.
IT'S HAPPENED TO HIM! HE'S GONE MAD!

GOPAL BOUGHT THE HILSA-FISH AND STARTED WALKING TOWARDS THE PALACE.
MOTHER, LOOK AT THAT MAN! ISN'T HE COMICAL?
HE MUST BE A MADMAN.
HUSH! I THINK HE'S A MYSTIC.
WHEN GOPAL REACHED THE COURT—
WHAT DO YOU WANT?
I WANT TO SEE THE KING!
YOU CAN'T SEE THE KING! GET AWAY WITH YOU!
GOPAL BEGAN TO DANCE AND SING LOUDLY.

INSIDE THE PALACE—
I WANT TO SEE THE KING. LET ME IN!
THE MAN IS CRAZY!
THROW HIM OUT AT ONCE!
BRING THAT MAN TO ME AT ONCE!
YES, YOUR MAJESTY.
GOPAL WAS BROUGHT BEFORE THE KING.
IT'S GOPAL!
THE MAN HAS LOST HIS MIND!
I THINK IT'S ONE OF HIS CRAZY JOKES.

ALL RIGHT, GOPAL. OUT WITH IT! WHY ARE YOU DRESSED UP IN THIS RIDICULOUS FASHION ?
YOUR MAJESTY, YOU SEEM TO HAVE FORGOTTEN SOMETHING!
FORGOTTEN SOMETHING ?
STRANGELY ENOUGH NO ONE SEEMS TO BE INTERESTED IN HILSA-FISH TODAY! FROM THE MARKET TO THE PALACE AND IN THE COURT, NOT A SOUL HAS SPOKEN A WORD ABOUT HILSA-FISH!
ONLY THEN DID THE KING REMEMBER THE CHALLENGE HE HAD THROWN TO GOPAL.
HA! HA! WELL GOPAL, CONGRATULATIONS! YOU HAVE ACHIEVED THE IMPOSSIBLE ONCE AGAIN!

GOPAL COUNTS THE STARS
YOU HAVEN'T BEEN LISTENING, YOUR MAJESTY. AND THAT WAS ONE OF MY BEST JOKES!
WILL YOU LEAVE ME ALONE! I AM IN NO MOOD FOR YOUR JOKES.
I SEE. THEN IT MUST BE THE NAWAB AGAIN. WHAT IS IT THIS TIME?
OH, NOTHING MUCH. HE ONLY WANTS A CENSUS OF ALL THE STARS IN THE SKY! WHAT DOES HE THINK I AM? A MAGICIAN?

LEAVE IT TO ME, YOUR MAJESTY ? IF I COULD MEASURE THE EARTH, I CAN COUNT THE STARS, TOO! ALL I NEED IS A FLOCK OF SHEEP.
A FLOCK OF SHEEP ? WHAT HAVE SHEEP TO DO WITH STARS ?
YOU'LL FIND OUT, BY AND BY, YOUR MAJESTY.
GOPAL TOOK THE SHEEP TO MURSHIDABAD AND WAITED OUTSIDE THE MOSQUE.
AH ! HERE COMES THE NAWAB FOR HIS MORNING PRAYERS.
TWO THOUSAND ONE HUNDRED AND FIFTY-FOUR. TWO THOUSAND ONE HUNDRED AND FIFTY-FIVE...
WHAT'S THAT FELLOW UP TO ?
...TWO THOUSAND ONE HUNDRED AND FIFTY-SIX. TWO THOUSAND ONE HUNDRED AND...
HEY, YOU !

OH, NO! I'LL HAVE TO START ALL OVER AGAIN!
START WHAT ALL OVER AGAIN?
COUNTING THE HAIRS ON THIS FLOCK OF SHEEP, YOUR EXCELLENCY.
ARE YOU CRAZY? WHAT A FOOLISH THING TO ATTEMPT.
ISN'T IT LESS FOOLISH THAN COUNTING THE STARS, YOUR EXCELLENCY?
COUNTING THE STARS? AHEM! ER...I SUPPOSE IT IS RATHER POINTLESS. THERE ARE A LOT MORE USEFUL THINGS TO DO. ER...YOU MAY GO...I'LL SPEAK TO THE MAHARAJA.
THANK YOU, YOUR EXCELLENCY. THANK YOU.

AMAR CHITRA KATHA

Illustrated Classics from India

Amar Chitra Katha is a collection of over 430 illustrated classics that retell stories from Indian mythology, history, folktale and legend, through the fascinating medium of comics. The Amar Chitra Katha comics are family heirlooms, passed down from generation to generation, creating unbreakable bonds with our common cultural heritage.

Mythology

- ☐ 501 Krishna
- ☐ 502 Hanuman
- ☐ 510 Buddha
- ☐ 511 Savitri
- ☐ 512 Tales of Vishnu
- ☐ 520 Tales of Narada
- ☐ 524 Indra and Shibi
- ☐ 525 Tales of Arjuna
- ☐ 531 Karna
- ☐ 533 Abhimanyu
- ☐ 547 Garuda
- ☐ 565 Drona
- ☐ 566 Surya
- ☐ 567 Indra and Shachi
- ☐ 570 Dasharatha
- ☐ 571 Dhruva and Ashtavakra
- ☐ 572 Ancestors of Rama
- ☐ 589 Krishna and Shishupala
- ☐ 592 Ghatotkacha
- ☐ 612 Urvashi
- ☐ 663 Aniruddha

Folktales

- ☐ 507 Nala Damayanti
- ☐ 523 Raman of Tenali
- ☐ 543 Jataka Tales: Monkey Stories
- ☐ 553 Jataka Tales: Jackal Stories
- ☐ 554 Jataka Tales: Elephant Stories
- ☐ 555 Jataka Tales: Deer Stories
- ☐ 557 Birbal the Witty
- ☐ 558 Birbal the Clever
- ☐ 559 Birbal the Just
- ☐ 578 Kesari the Flying Thief
- ☐ 580 The Inimitable Birbal
- ☐ 581 Raman the Matchless Wit
- ☐ 584 Gopal the Jester
- ☐ 587 Birbal the Genius
- ☐ 607 A Bag of Gold Coins
- ☐ 621 Udayana
- ☐ 625 Battle of Wits
- ☐ 659 Devi Choudhurani
- ☐ 664 King Kusha
- ☐ 667 Bikal the Terrible
- ☐ 713 The Fool's Disciples

History

- ☐ 508 Chanakya
- ☐ 536 Ashoka
- ☐ 563 Rana Pratap
- ☐ 568 Vikramaditya
- ☐ 636 Krishnadeva Raya
- ☐ 603 Akbar
- ☐ 604 Prithviraj Chauhan
- ☐ 606 Rani Durgavati
- ☐ 627 Harsha
- ☐ 630 Rana Sanga
- ☐ 539 Rani of Jhansi
- ☐ 648 Samudra Gupta
- ☐ 676 Rana Kumbha
- ☐ 682 Tanaji
- ☐ 685 Chand Bibi
- ☐ 701 Noor Jahan
- ☐ 704 Jallianwala Bagh
- ☐ 722 Megasthenes
- ☐ 696 The Historic City of Delhi
- ☐ 725 Sultana Razia
- ☐ 734 Banda Bahadur

Biography

- ☐ 517 Vivekananda
- ☐ 535 Mirabai
- ☐ 632 Vidyasagar
- ☐ 544 Subhas Chandra Bose
- ☐ 548 Rabindranath Tagore
- ☐ 551 Tulsidas
- ☐ 563 Rana Pratap
- ☐ 564 Shivaji
- ☐ 608 Bhagat Singh
- ☐ 611 Babasaheb Ambedkar
- ☐ 735 JRD Tata
- ☐ 631 Chaitanya Mahaprabhu
- ☐ 699 Jagadis Chandra Bose
- ☐ 645 Lokamanya Tilak
- ☐ 647 Lal Bahadur Shastri
- ☐ 650 Mahatma Gandhi
- ☐ 678 Veer Savarkar
- ☐ 736 Kalpana Chawla
- ☐ 693 Jayaprakash Narayan
- ☐ 700 Jawaharlal Nehru
- ☐ 732 Swami Chinmayananda

Start your collection today! Visit us on www.AmarChitraKatha.com

IBH
INDIA BOOK HOUSE
Mahalaxmi Chambers, 5th floor, 22 Bhulabhai Desai Road, Mumbai 400 026, India
Tel +91 22 23523827 Fax +91 22 23538406 Email info@amarchitrakatha.com